Avocado with carrot salad

MOLLY LYONS BAR-DAVID

JEWISH

cooking for pleasure

PAUL HAMLYN · LONDON

FOR
My Granddaughters Three . . .

GEFFEN, the Vine
DEGANIT, the Cornflower
INBAR, the Amber Jewel

whose parents are helping to make
the desert of Israel blossom as the rose at
Kibbutz Yotvata by the Red Sea of Elat

PHOTOGRAPHER   Christian Délu
ILLUSTRATORS   Jill Mackley, Gay John Galsworthy
DESIGNER   Veronica Mathew

Reprinted 1967 — in France by Brodard et Taupin
Published by PAUL HAMLYN LIMITED
DRURY HOUSE · RUSSELL STREET · LONDON WC 2
T 1538

CONTENTS

INTRODUCTION

My apologies to my dear husband, Jaap Bar-David, and my darling daughters, Varda, Giela, Ziona and Sharon, for the ordeals they suffered as a tasting panel in my testing kitchen.

My heartfelt thanks to my editor, Miss Renée Hellman, for cheerful encouragement and her hard labour and her help in converting my USA measures into such exact UK measures.

My admiration to Monsieur Christian Délu and his assistant Madame Thérèse Rebessé, who travelled from Paris to Israel to photograph the dishes for this book.

My appreciation and thanks to the following for the loan of their beautiful native and antique handicrafts, embroideries, weaving, glassware, ceramics, metalware and other lovely things used as props for the photos in this book:

WIZO SHOPS OF HOME INDUSTRIES, ALLENBY ROAD, TEL AVIV
BATSHEVA CRAFTS CORPORATION LTD., FRUG STREET, TEL AVIV

MASKIT DEVELOPMENT OF HOME CRAFTS, BEN YEHUDA STREET, TEL AVIV
J. &. R. CERAMICS, MAGAL STREET, SAVYON
GELBERG HOUSEHOLD WARE, SHOPPING CENTRE, SAVYON

My deep gratitude and praise to the fifty-four women of Savyon WIZO who spent three weeks cooking the many dishes for photography in this book. Double thanks are due to Mrs. Shula Braudo and Mrs. Talma Zakai who were in charge of this 'Operation Cooking'; to them and to Mrs. Helma Shepherd, Mrs. Florie Kwitz, Mrs. Sybil Levine and Mrs. Malka Azaryah, additional thanks for turning their homes into studios for this task.

I am happy that Paul Hamlyn Ltd. made a generous contribution to WIZO for this task, as such funds will go to vital charitable projects. My thanks again, to one and all.

MOLLY LYONS BAR-DAVID, SAVYON, ISRAEL

THE ORIGIN OF JEWISH COOKING

The cuisine of peoples the world over is usually born of the bountiful products of their land and the climate of their country.

Though cast out from their homeland, and dispersed over all the world for over two thousand years, the Jewish people nonetheless do have a cooking of their own, with different nuances in East and West. These subtle changes are due to local products, and the influence of the dishes in their locales. This unity is chiefly due to the fact that Jewish cooking emanates from religious festivals, biblical symbolism, the requirements of the kosher laws, and traditional associations linked with national longings, hopes and prayers. For a festival some dishes, like

gefilte fish, were created out of poverty of the Jewish masses, when a good thing had to stretch a long way.

The biblical admonition 'Thou shalt not cook the kid in its mother's milk' is the humane law which led to the separation of dairy and meat foods, and even the dishes were separate as in those days pottery absorbed both milk and gravy. Nowadays medicine has discovered that swine harbour a dangerous worm, that shrimps are poisonous in certain seasons . . . points which may have led to the forbidding of such foods to Jewish people in biblical times. Even the salting of meat makes good sense in the hot summer of Israel, for salt was a great aid in stopping

spoilage in the days when there was no other way of preservation for a day or two. Jewry has clung to these culinary laws, even in the face of the modern guards of refrigeration and scientific caution, as a way of Jewish identification. But kosher problems are being coped with in modern cooking: in Israel we have developed a *pareve*, non-dairy ice-cream which may be taken with meat meals; in the United States there is a chicken à la king without cream, and in Greece a kosher moussaka is made without cheese . . . all almost identical in taste with the original dairy-enriched ingredients in the dish. The ruling that on the Sabbath no fire may be kindled (for in olden days it was quite a chore) is the reason that food is not cooked, but may be kept hot, on the Holy Day of Rest. This law created the *cholent*. It is a dish of meat, dumpling, pulse and vegetable that is put to cook on Friday evening, left to simmer and mellow on a very low heat until after Synagogue service on the Sabbath, and then eaten for lunch.

The Sabbath *kugels* (puddings) sprang from Germanic countries and one is referred to in writings eight hundred years ago. The *farfel kugel* is recorded in 1500 in Polish writings when the name of this pasta was still called *frimselles*. The loaves of bread on the Sabbath table are biblical symbols of the shew bread on altars in ancient times. Two loaves are used to symbolize the double portion of manna which was collected for the Sabbath in the desert on Friday. On Rosh Hashono — the Jewish New Year — the loaves are sweet and round, as a wish for a sweet year and as a symbol of the circle of fate. Often these loaves are braided to look like crowns, for the crown of the Lord's Kingdom, and the silver crowns on the Torah Scrolls. Ladders and birds are on the loaves in some Jewish communities, symbols for their prayers to ascend more easily to heaven.

Apples and honey, and dishes made of them, are on the Rosh Hashono table as evidence of the sweetness of the year, and of the harvest which we have survived to taste. Carrot *tzimmis* is a hopeful symbol of prosperity, being golden and coin-shaped. The head of a sheep or a fish is on the table of Sephardic Jewish households as reminders of the promise that Israel shall be at the head and not at the tail of the nations of the world. Many vegetables appear on Sephardic tables with a play on words for good omens and wishes.

The harvest festival of Succot features *sarmis* in Oriental households, chopped meat and rice rolled up in grape leaves, reminiscent of the Judean vineyards. *Strudels* — pastries of dried fruits — may be served to exemplify the seven fruits of the Bible. *Fluden* for centuries served on Simhat Torah (the last day of Succot week) is reminiscent of the pressed cakes of fruit in the Bible. In some countries *fluden* comes to the table with white flowers, symbolic of the Bible's purity, for on this day the last and first chapters are read in the service.

The festival of Hanuka is celebrated with pancakes, the fried fritters being reminiscent of the oil found in the Temple. In Western lands potatoes form the batter, while in most other lands a flour dough is used. In Israel the *soofganiyot* are the treat of Hanuka. It is a two-thousand-year-old Holy Land recipe, almost identical with the Hellenic period *soofganin* (meaning sponge) recorded in the Maccabean era, when spongy dough balls were deep fried and dipped in honey.

Tu B'Shvat features fruits and fruit dishes, for this 'New Year of the Trees' was created in the days of the Mishna as a national festival to bind us to the tree-planting season in the Holy Land, though our scattered people were far from the ancient homeland.

Purim, 'a day of joy and feasting and gaiety, a day of food gifts and giving to the poor',

celebrates the rescue of our people from the villainous plan of Haman in Persia, to destroy our people there, some two thousand, five hundred years ago. As the name *Haman* sounds like *mohn* (poppy-seed), many dishes of poppy-seed mock him on this day. *Hamantaschen* (Haman's pockets) are filled with poppy-seed to remind us of Haman's pockets full of silver which, with villain's cunning, he offered to King Ahashverus. *Oznei Haman* (Haman's ears) are twirly fried pastries to mock the criminal's ears which were cut off on his way to the scaffold, as was done to all condemned in those days. *Povidl* — a plum jam — goes into the making of many Purim pastries, in memory of the rescue of our people from a pogrom in Bohemia two hundred and thirty-five years ago, when a plum jam merchant was saved from death at the last moment.

As leaven is forbidden on the Passover, many dishes are made of matzo and matzo meal to replace ordinary flour. Thus the *knaidle* dumplings and *chremslach* fritters have become national dishes. Horseradish relish, in memory of the bitterness we suffered as slaves in Egypt, has become a popular condiment all year round. Lamb, symbolic of the sheep's blood on the doorposts to keep away the angel of death just prior to our exodus from Egypt, is served on Seder Night in most Eastern Jewish homes.

Shavuot, the Pentecost festival of the first fruits, is the day of dairy dishes and floral symbols. Not only are synagogues and homes decorated with blooms, but in some Eastern communities desserts are garnished with roses. In Afghanistan Shavuot is called the 'Feast of Roses'. Cakes are often shaped like Mount Sinai, with a topping for the cloud, where the Commandments were given to us. Dairy dishes such as cheese *blintzes*, cheese *knishes* and cheese cakes have become all year favourites, though on this day they symbolize the white purity of the Commandments.

Legend also records that the reason for eating cheese on Shavuot is because we waited for so long on Mount Sinai that the milk curdled, and we were left with white cheese for cooking.

Newer foods in Jewish cookery have sprung up in Israel. During the siege of Jerusalem in 1948 we subsisted on the wild purslane (*halamit* in Hebrew) in the fields. This plant is referred to in the suffering Book of Job: 'Is there any taste in the juice of a purslane?' And indeed the *halamit* even today has the name of the 'Bread of the Hungry' among Arabs. Since our liberation, purslane pancakes are symbolically served on Independence Day. As this festival is usually celebrated outdoors in picnic spirit, the *shashlik* has also been adopted as a national dish, not only because it is popular in all the Middle East, but because the lamb is grilled on wooden embers in the way of the altar sacrifices of biblical days. Even herbs and spices are much the same in the dish!

Jewish cuisine has not only adapted the dishes of many lands, altering them to conform to kosher laws, but even the names have often remained in their original language, so that terms such as *strudel* or *torte* or *pierogi* or *borsht* are familiar to Jewish vocabulary even though the dish is not the same as the original Gentile one. Dishes created by Jewish housewives in the Diaspora have Yiddish names or Ladino names depending on whether the cooks were Ashkenazic or Sephardic Jews. The Ashkenazic Jews come chiefly from Central and Eastern Europe and so their Yiddish language is much like German. The Sephardic Jews come originally from Spain (and with the Inquisition in the 15th century fled to the Mediterranean areas and as far west as Holland in Europe) and so their Ladino tongue is much like Spanish. Though both communities have dispersed all over the world, each group has retained its own cooking as well as other cultural features.

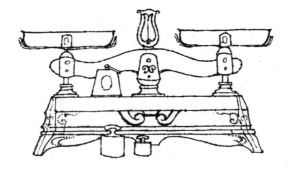

WEIGHTS AND MEASURES

Weights throughout the book are given in lb. and oz. Capacity measure in Imperial pints and fractions thereof, with small amounts in spoon measures. For the benefit of American readers liquid ingredients have been given to the nearest U.S. standard cup measure. These follow the English measure — i.e. 1 pint (U.S. 2½ cups). All spoon measures refer to the British Standards Institution specification. All measures are levelled off to the rim of the spoon. To measure fractions of spoons use the small measures provided in measuring sets or divide the level spoon. The American standard measuring spoons are slightly smaller in capacity than the British standard measuring spoons. The proportion, however, is similar in that 3 American standard teaspoons equal 1 tablespoon.

METRIC EQUIVALENTS

It is difficult to convert to French measures with absolute accuracy, but 1 oz. is equal to approximately 30 grammes, 2 lb. 3 oz. to 1 kilogramme. For liquid measure, approximately 1¾ English pints may be regarded as equal to 1 litre; ½ pint to 3 decilitres (scant); 3½ fluid oz. to 1 decilitre.

OVEN TEMPERATURES

DESCRIPTION OF OVEN	APPROXIMATE TEMPERATURE CENTRE OF OVEN °F.	THERMOSTAT SETTING
Very Slow or	200—250	¼ = 240
Very Cool		½ = 265
		1 = 290
Slow or Cool	250—300	2 = 310
Very Moderate	300—350	3 = 335
Moderate	350—375	4 = 350
Moderately Hot		5 = 375
to Hot	375—400	6 = 400
Hot to Very Hot	425—450	7 = 425
Very Hot	450—500	8 = 450
		9 = 470

Note THIS TABLE IS AN APPROXIMATE GUIDE ONLY. DIFFERENT MAKES OF COOKER VARY AND IF YOU ARE IN ANY DOUBT ABOUT THE SETTING IT IS AS WELL TO REFER TO THE MANUFACTURER'S TEMPERATURE CHART

HORS-D'OEUVRE

Appetizers in the Western world are relatively new — judging in terms of millennia and not centuries. Since time immemorial, however, the Jews have celebrated the Seder with symbolic appetizers in the long pre-meal Passover table ceremony. Haroset (see page 146) is emblematic of the mortar on which we worked as slaves in Egypt; celery, lettuce, parsley, are symbols of the green harvest; eggs in salt water, for life and tears which we have experienced; horseradish-matzo sandwich bites in memory of the bitterness we suffered: all these Seder-plate tasters evoke not only historic memories, but also arouse the appetite for the dinner that follows.

Modern Jewish cuisine has also adopted and adapted appetizers from over the world where we were dispersed for two thousand years. The Mediterranean felafel and humos snack, generally eaten in a pita sandwich on the street, has become a popular cocktail party bite and dip in Israel. Herring, once the pauper's food on Jewish tables of Eastern Europe, now makes a delightful introduction to a meal, and can also be put on crackers to enjoy with a drink before dinner. So relished are the first courses in this section that many of them — like ikre and gehakte hirring and aubergines — have become spreads for canapés and a new word has just been introduced into the ancient Hebrew language to name them: 'Dig-Dag' is the term, and it means a 'tickling tempter for the palate'.

FELAFEL

CHICK PEA QUENELLE

(Also illustrated in colour on page 19)
Cooking time about 10 minutes
To serve 6—8

You will need

8 oz. chick peas
4 tablespoons burghul (cracked wheat)
3 cloves garlic, chopped
1 teaspoon salt
3 tablespoons flour
1 teaspoon cumin
$\frac{1}{4}$ teaspoon chilli pepper
$\frac{1}{4}$ teaspoon coriander
1 egg
deep fat for frying

Soak chick peas for 12 hours and then put through the mincer.
Soak burghul for 1 hour, and if coarsely cracked put it through the mincer as well.
Mix all the ingredients together.
Shape into balls (about $\frac{3}{4}$ inch in diameter).
Fry in very hot deep fat until brown.
Reheat before serving.

This Israeli tidbit is an ideal cocktail snack.

Note

Felafel is sold from kiosks in Israel, in pita (see page 55) pancake-bread envelopes, dressed with tahina (see page 18) sauce, schoog (see page 110) relish, mint salad (see page 89) and sauerkraut (see page 109) or with cucumber dill pickles (see page 112).

Chick pea quenelle

HUMOUS V'TEHINA

CHICK PEA
AND SESAME APPETIZER

(Illustrated in colour on page 19)
Cooking time   about 2 hours
To serve   6—8

You will need

13¼ oz. chick peas
2 cloves garlic, crushed *
juice 1 lemon
salt to taste
pepper or cayenne to taste
1 lb. tahina paste (see page 18)

FOR GARNISH

3 tablespoons olive oil
3 tablespoons chopped parsley
sprinkling paprika or cayenne
vinegar pickles
olives
parsley sprigs

* You can add more garlic if you wish.

Soak the raw chick peas overnight and then cook them until the skins come off. Save a few, purée the rest while hot and stir in the remaining ingredients. The consistency of the chick peas should be very heavy mayonnaise. You may require some hot water in order to dilute to the desired thickness. Serve like tahina (see page 18) flattened on small plates with a swirl of olive oil, sprinkling of parsley, paprika or cayenne, parsley sprigs and a side dish of pickles and olives. This can be served as a first course at dinner or as a dip with an aperitif.

HIRRING FORSCHMAK
HERRING APPETIZERS

Herring appetizers can be served in many ways. But first you must soak the herring overnight and then, if you wish, fillet it or cut into pieces. Dress it in any of the following ways:

1 With vinegar, oil, pepper, sliced onions and black olives

2 With white wine (set aside for a few hours to marinate) to which a little sugar and vinegar or lemon juice have been added

3 With olive oil and lemon juice and tomato halves for garnish

4 With sour cream or mayonnaise or both mixed together

5 A piece of filleted herring impaled with a toothpick on an apple slice

6 Fillets rolled up with a dill pickle and sauerkraut for filling. These are then called 'Rollmops'

Herring appetizers

Stuffed fowl neck

HELZEL

STUFFED FOWL NECK

Cooking time   about 1 hour
To serve   2

You will need

1 skin of chicken neck *

STUFFING

2 tablespoons matzo meal or semolina or
   breadcrumbs
2 tablespoons soy flour or ordinary flour
6 tablespoons chopped onion
salt and generous amount pepper
1½ oz. raw chicken fat or margarine
¼ teaspoon chicken soup powder (optional)

* This can also be made of chicken, turkey, goose
   or duck necks.

Mix all ingredients for stuffing and loosely fill the
skin of the chicken neck. Sew up both ends. Roast
next to meat or chicken, basting with gravy in the
pan from time to time. The helzel needs the same
roasting time as the fowl.
Helzel is usually cut and served on a small plate
with a little gravy.

VARIATIONS

Turkish Jews use white bread instead of breadcrumbs and flour, and they add chopped walnuts to
the filling.
Oriental Jews add saffron and cinnamon to the
filling, and in place of breadcrumbs they add
ground meat or chopped hard-boiled eggs.

TZIHBILLIS MIT AYER
ONION WITH EGG DRESSING

Cooking time   20 minutes
To serve   6

You will need

1 lb. sweet onions
5 hard-boiled egg yolks
2½ oz. chicken or goose fat
salt and pepper to taste

Dice the onions and mix with the remaining ingredients. If you wish, 1 onion can be lightly fried
in the fat until just golden and mixed with the
sweet raw onion.
This is a beloved Russian-Jewish dish.

GEHAKTE HIRRING

CHOPPED HERRING

No cooking
To serve   10

You will need

3 salt herrings
2 slices white bread
water
2 onions
1 carrot or parsley root or celery root
2 hard-boiled eggs
1 apple
2 teaspoons sugar
½ teaspoon cinnamon (optional)
¼ teaspoon pepper
3 tablespoons oil
4 tablespoons mild vinegar

TO GARNISH

black olives
green onions

Soak the herrings overnight, clean and fillet them.
Soak the bread in water and then squeeze out the
moisture. Put the herrings, bread, onions, carrot or
parsley root, eggs and apple through the mincer.
Add the remaining ingredients and mix well.
Garnish with olives and green onions.
This is an East-European appetizer that has gone
internationally Jewish.

Stuffed tomatoes

MEDYAHS
STUFFED TOMATOES

Cooking time 30 minutes
To serve 6

You will need

6 large tomatoes
1 lb. minced beef or lamb
2 onions, finely chopped
1 tablespoon olive oil
1 tablespoon breadcrumbs
1 tablespoon chopped parsley
water
2 eggs, beaten
⅛ teaspoon cinnamon *
salt and pepper

FOR DIPPING

1 egg, beaten
3 tablespoons flour
pinch salt
fat for frying

* Some Mediterranean Jewish communities use
  coriander or allspice instead of cinnamon in this
  dish.

Cut tomatoes in half, crosswise. Scoop out the pulp
and put it in a baking dish. Mix the beef with the
onion, oil, breadcrumbs, parsley, 1 tablespoon
water, eggs, cinnamon, salt and pepper. Fill the
tomato shells with the meat mixture. Dip the stuffed
tomatoes in the egg and then into the salted flour.
Fry the tomato, meat side down, for 1 minute.
Put tomatoes into baking dish, meat side up on
tomato pulp. Add a scant ¼ pint (U.S. ½ cup) water

to the baking dish and bake for about 30 minutes
at 400°F. or Gas Mark 6. This Sephardic (Spanish)
Jewish dish is often referred to as an 'Old Jerusalem' recipe.

PIPIKLACH
GIZZARDS

Cooking time 1 hour
To serve 6

You will need

30 gizzards
water to cover
salt and pepper
2 onions, chopped
5 tablespoons chicken fat (or oil plus
   1 teaspoon chicken soup powder)

Cover gizzards with water and simmer until tender.
When almost all the water has evaporated add the
remaining ingredients and cook until gizzards are
brown but not hard. This can be served on rice for
a main course.
This dish is so loved that 'Pipiklach' is the diminu-
tive term of 'Pipiks'.

GIPIKILTI HIRRING
MARINATED HERRING

Cooking time 1 minute
To make 24 appetizers

You will need

4 salt herrings
⅘ pint (U.S. 2 cups) white vinegar
   (mild or diluted)
2 onions, sliced thinly
2 bay leaves
8 whole peppers
1 teaspoon celery seed

Soak herrings overnight. Clean and cut each into
6 pieces — or if you prefer, fillet and then cut the
herring. Bring the vinegar to the boil with the remaining ingredients. Cool the marinade thoroughly
and then pour over the herring. Set aside to marinate for one day before using. This can be served
as it is or with a little sour cream mixed with some
of the marinade as a dressing.
This appetizer keeps for weeks in the refrigerator.

13

LIBERLACH MIT TZIHBILLIS

CHICKEN LIVERS AND ONIONS

Cooking time   20—30 minutes
To serve   6

You will need

12 chicken livers or goose livers *
12 onions, thinly sliced
4 oz. chicken fat
salt and pepper
mushrooms (optional)

* For Kashrut laws, to rid the meat of blood, livers
  must be grilled first.

Before grilling dip livers in cold water to prevent
hardening.
While the livers are grilling, fry the onions in the
chicken fat and season with salt and pepper. Add
sliced mushrooms if desired. When livers are
sufficiently grilled add them to the pan and
smother them in the onions. Cook a few minutes
more and serve hot.

GEHAKTE LEBER

CHOPPED LIVER

Cooking time   20—30 minutes
To serve   6

You will need

1 lb. poultry or beef liver
8 oz. onions, chopped
3 tablespoons poultry fat
3 hard-boiled eggs
salt and pepper to taste

TO GARNISH

lettuce leaves
tomato halves

Grill the liver until all the blood has dripped off
(a kosher requirement). Fry the onions in poultry
fat. Put liver, onions and eggs through the mincer.
Add seasoning. Serve with tomato halves on lettuce
leaves.

One of the most international of Jewish appetizers.

Chopped liver; chicken livers and onions

PITCHA

JELLIED CALF'S FOOT

Cooking time   2—3 hours
To serve   6—8

You will need

1 calf's foot, sawn and split
about 4 pints (U.S. 10 cups) water
1 bay leaf
3 cloves garlic, chopped
2 teaspoons salt
⅛ teaspoon white pepper
¼ teaspoon allspice
scant ¼ pint (U.S. ½ cup) white wine or
    citrus vinegar
3 hard-boiled eggs, sliced

Bring the calf's foot to the boil with the water and
remove the froth which comes to the top. Add the
bay leaf. Simmer for a few hours on a low heat until
all the meat and gristle can be removed from the
bone. Cut up the gristle and add to the strained
liquid with the garlic, salt, pepper, allspice and
white wine or vinegar and boil for a further
10 minutes. Put the egg slices in the bottom of
a mould, cover with gristle and spoon on the liquid.
Chill until firm.

Note

This dish can also be served hot in its liquid state,
as an unusually rich soup-like course. *Pitcha* is the
Russian-Jewish name of this dish, *Pilseh* the Rumanian title, and *Fisnoga* seems to be of Spanish origin.

Jellied calf's foot

HAZILIM MEMULAIM
AUBERGINES FILLED WITH MEAT

Cooking time 50 minutes
To serve 6

You will need

2 lb. aubergine (small variety)
8 oz. lamb, diced as small as possible
2 medium-sized onions, chopped
4 tablespoons cooking oil
1 teaspoon salt
¼ teaspoon black pepper
1 large tomato, peeled and chopped
3 tablespoons chopped parsley
2 teaspoons sugar
4 tablespoons melted margarine
2 dashes chilli powder or 1 teaspoon
    chilli sauce
5¼ oz. rice
3 tablespoons ground almonds
3 tablespoons tomato purée or ketchup
water

Cut aubergines in half lengthwise and scoop out almost all the flesh, without breaking the skin. Fry the meat, the cut up aubergine flesh and onion in half the oil. Remove from heat and add half the salt, pepper, tomato, parsley, half the sugar, 1 tablespoon of melted margarine and the chilli powder or chilli sauce. Add the rice, almonds and 1 tablespoon of tomato purée. Half fill the aubergines. With the remaining oil fry them in a shallow pan. Add water to reach the rim of the aubergine. Mix together and add the remaining margarine, another dash of chilli powder or sauce, the rest of the salt, sugar and tomato purée. Cook over medium heat for about 30 minutes, then remove to a baking dish and bake in a moderately hot oven (400°F. or Gas Mark 6) for about 20 minutes, basting from time to time.
This way of filling aubergine is worth the effort.

Note
Any filling which may remain, if too much of the aubergine is scooped out, can be baked separately in a casserole between layers of sliced aubergine and covered with chopped tomatoes or any desired tomato sauce.

KISHKE
STUFFED BEEF CASINGS OF DERMA

Cooking time 2 hours
To serve 6

You will need

12—16 inches beef intestines
    (depending on width)
6 oz. flour
2 tablespoons semolina
2 large onions, diced
1½ teaspoons table salt
½ teaspoon pepper
¼ teaspoon celery salt

Scrape the shiny side of the beef casings and wash thoroughly. Mix together all the other ingredients. Sew up one end of the beef intestines and proceed to fill the casing, pushing it back as you continue filling, until the whole shiny side is again exposed. Be sure not to overstuff the intestines as the filling expands. Sew up the other end. Place in pot with a roast, or on a bed of onions, or along with any cholent (see pages 45, 80). Cover with water and cook for about 2 hours on a medium heat until golden and most of the water absorbed.

Note
This dish must be served hot, either in gravy from the roast or with horseradish relish (see page 109). This was the poor Jews' food which developed into a luscious dish in Central Europe.

IKRE

KOSHER CAVIAR

No cooking
To serve 6

You will need

8 oz. raw fish roe
about ⅝ pint (U.S. 2 cups) salad oil
salt and pepper to taste
2 slices white bread
water
scant ¼ pint (U.S. ½ cup) lemon juice

TO GARNISH

finely chopped sweet onions
black olives
parsley

Cover the fish roe with a little of the oil and refrigerate for 24 hours. Remove membrane from roe
and stir up, adding the remaining oil slowly as you
beat the mixture. A mixture like mayonnaise will
be formed. Add salt and pepper. Remove the
crusts from the bread and dip in water, then
squeeze out the liquid. Add the crumbled bread and
continue beating, slowly adding the lemon juice.
Garnish the side of the dish with chopped onion,
black olives and parsley.

This appetizer is a Rumanian-Jewish delicacy.

Kosher caviar

GEZER HAI B'AVOCADO

AVOCADO WITH CARROT SALAD

(Illustrated in colour on frontispiece)
No cooking
To serve 8

You will need

1 lb. fresh carrots
juice 3 oranges
juice ½ lemon
salt and sugar to taste
dash ginger
2 avocado pears
8 anchovies

Coarsely grate the carrots. Cover with the orange
and lemon juice, adding sugar and salt to taste, with
a dash of ginger for piquancy. Refrigerate for at
least 6 hours so that the carrots absorb the flavour of
the juices. You can use the juice for other purposes
later on.
Quarter the avocado pears lengthwise. Fill with
the drained carrots and top with an anchovy.

This carrot mixture is called 'living carrots' and
can also be used as a separate salad.

VARIATION

The grated carrots can also be served on lettuce or
in lemon baskets garnished with a sprig of mint.

GREBEN

CRACKLINGS

Cooking time 30—45 minutes

You will need

goose, chicken or any fowl fat
skin of any fowl
salt
onions as desired, diced
water to just cover

Cut the fat and skin into 1-inch squares or cubes.
Put the fat, skin, salt, onions and water on low heat
so that the fat melts and the cracklings do not burn.
After some time the water will evaporate and the
cracklings and the onions will begin to brown and
crisp in the fat. Remove when brown. Drain the
fat for separate use. Cracklings can be stored for
months in a cool place.

Cracklings are served with dishes such as radish salad, or with chopped liver or chopped eggs or on their own with fresh white bread.

GEHAKTE AYEHR
CHOPPED EGGS

No cooking
To serve 6

You will need

8 hard-boiled eggs
2½ oz. sweet onion
1 teaspoon salt
¼ teaspoon pepper
4 tablespoons chopped poultry cracklings * or
3 tablespoons chicken fat or oil plus
  ½ teaspoon chicken soup powder

FOR GARNISH

lettuce
tomato slices
black olives
sliced cucumbers

* Cracklings are made by rendering the skin and fat of fowl (see page 16).

Chopped eggs

Mash the hard-boiled eggs. Chop the onion. Into the eggs work in the onion, salt, pepper and cracklings.
Serve on lettuce and garnish with tomato slices, black olives and sliced cucumbers.

This is a favourite Jewish appetizer from Poland.

HIRRING SALAT
HERRING SALAD

Cooking time about 30 minutes
To serve 6

You will need

2 herrings
8 oz. potatoes
1 dill pickle, diced
8 oz. apples, diced
1 tablespoon chopped green onion
1 teaspoon sugar
scant ¼ pint (U.S. ½ cup) mayonnaise
scant ¼ pint (U.S. ½ cup) sour cream
4 tablespoons vinegar
1 tablespoon chopped parsley and/or dill
pepper to taste

FOR GARNISH

lettuce
tomato wedges
black olives

Soak herrings overnight, clean, fillet and cut into small pieces.
Cook the potatoes and dice them.
Dice the dill pickle and dice the apples.
Mix the potato, pickle, apples and onions with the herring.
Then mix together the sugar, mayonnaise, sour cream, vinegar, chopped parsley and/or dill and gently add to the salad.
Serve on lettuce, garnished with tomato wedges, and black olives.

VARIATIONS

Add diced celery stalk, chopped sweet red and green peppers. Another alternative is to add 2 hard-boiled eggs.

17

TAHINA

SESAME PASTE APPETIZER OR COCKTAIL DIP

No cooking
To serve   6—8

You will need

5¼ oz. sesame seeds
⅖ pint (U.S. 1 cup) water
2 cloves garlic
juice 2 lemons
1 teaspoon salt
pinch cayenne

TO GARNISH

3 tablespoons olive oil
3 tablespoons chopped parsley
sprinkling paprika
olives

Put the sesame seeds, water, garlic and lemon juice through a blender to make a paste. Add more water if needed, to achieve mayonnaise-like consistency. Add the seasoning. Serve flattened on little plates, garnished with a swirl of olive oil, sprinkling of parsley and paprika, and centred with olives.

Note
When diluted with vinegar, this becomes a dressing, sauce, or dip. If used as a cocktail dip, omit garnish.

SMETINI HIRRING MIT VINE

HERRING IN WINE AND SOUR CREAM

Cooking time   1 minute
To make   30 appetizers

You will need

6 milt herrings
scant ¼ pint (U.S. ½ cup) white wine
    vinegar
2 onions, thinly sliced
3 bay leaves
1 teaspoon peppercorns
scant ¼ pint (U.S. ½ cup) dry white wine
2 tablespoons sugar
⅖ pint (U.S. 1 cup) sour cream

Clean and soak the herrings overnight. Soak the white milt roes separately for 12 hours.
Bring the vinegar to the boil with the onions, bay leaves and peppercorns. Add the wine and heat but do not boil. Sieve the roes so that you eliminate the membranes and mix with the sugar and sour cream. Add to the onion mixture.
Fillet the herring and cut into pieces. Layer with the sauce in a jar and marinate for a day. Keep refrigerated.

This is a very delicate appetizer, despite the high herring flavour.

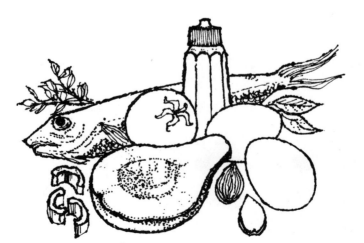

Chick pea quenelle; chick pea and sesame appetizer

Sour cream beetroot soup

SOUPS AND SOUP GARNISHES

MARAKIM V'KISHUTEI MARAK

Gilderneh yoich — golden soup — is a Sabbath Eve chicken broth on all Jewish tables; its garnish can be noodles or rice or kreplach or knaidlach or balletjes or what you will, but the soup itself is the popular treat. Its delicately rich taste is due not only to the flavour of onions and carrots and other root vegetables, but to the whole bird that goes into its making, and the fact that the rounds of golden fat which float on the surface are not removed. This soup is so traditional that many a Yiddish writer and poet laud its aroma, flavour and glint, in tales of grand wedding feasts or in praising the Sabbath dinner.

The biblical promise that our desert would blossom as the rose is coming true in Israel. So much so that our fruits are bountiful enough to have gone into the creating and popularizing of refreshing fruit soups. These soups — almost always served chilled — not only open a meal at table, but sometimes they are served as a dessert. They can be a porch summer drink, or a substitute for an aperitif, or a table drink in a glass with the meal. It depends on the contents, thick or thin, sweet or piquant, wined or spiced. Every housewife is an adventuress in making her own combinations, using any of these fruits of our soil . . . apples, apricots, avocadoes, bananas, custard apples, clementines, dates, figs, feijoas, grapes, guavas, grapefruit, granadilla, kumquats, lemons, loquats, mulberries, mangoes, melons, mandarins, oranges, peaches, pears, persimmons, plums, pitangos, pomegranates, prickly-pears, quinces, raspberries, rhubarb, strawberries, water-melons, and others being grown in the testing stage.

YOICH MANDLEN
SOUP PASTE PUFFS

Cooking time   about 5 minutes
To serve   6 — 8

You will need

3 eggs, beaten slightly
3 teaspoons oil
6 oz. flour, sifted
$\frac{3}{4}$ teaspoon salt
$\frac{3}{4}$ teaspoon baking powder
deep fat for frying

Mix the eggs and oil together and then add the remaining ingredients.
Roll dough out into $\frac{1}{2}$-inch-thick cords and then cut into $\frac{1}{2}$-inch pieces with a floured knife. Fry in deep hot fat until golden and puffed.
Serve soup paste puffs in soup.

Note

Mandlen means almonds, but there are no nuts in this recipe.

Fruit soup

MARAK PEYROT
FRUIT SOUP

Cooking time   depends upon fruits used
To serve   10

You will need

1¾ lb. mixed chopped fresh fruits, or
   10¾ oz. dried fruits *
water
sugar as desired
1¼ pints (U.S. 3 cups) orange juice
lemon juice to taste
3 tablespoons cornflour
⅖ pint (U.S. 1 cup) dry white wine (optional)

FOR GARNISH

sour cream (optional)
mint sprigs (optional)

* Any fruits in season are used, such as apples,
quinces, strawberries, apricots, mulberries, figs,
cherries, grapes, guavas, melons, peaches, pears,
plums.

Cook the fruits until very soft, in 3½ pints (U.S.
8 cups) water. Add sugar as desired and cook a few
minutes more. Fruits may be left in pieces or mashed
through a sieve. Add the orange and lemon juice
and reheat. Dissolve the cornflour in a little water
and add to the fruit mixture. Boil for 1—2 minutes.
Chill. If you wish, wine may be added before
serving. Garnish, if you wish, with a spoonful of
sour cream or a sprig of mint.
Marak Peyrot is one of the most loved soups in Israel.

LOKSHEN
NOODLES

No cooking
To serve   8

You will need

1 lb. flour
4 eggs
2 tablespoons water

Sift flour into a mound. Make a well in the centre
and put in eggs and water. Work into a dough and
knead well. Roll out finely on to a floured board
and put sheets to dry on towels for about 30 minutes. Fold dough over lightly and cut into desired
widths with a sharp knife. Sprinkle noodles on to
floured cloths and leave to dry until hard.
Nowadays these noodles can be purchased com-
mercially in packages.

SCHAV
SORREL SUMMER SOUP

Cooking time   about 45 minutes
To serve   8

You will need

¾ oz. chopped parsley
1 lb. sorrel leaves, chopped
3¼ pints (U.S. 8 cups) soup stock
2 tablespoons lemon juice
3 tablespoons sugar
¼ teaspoon celery salt
salt and pepper to taste
⅖ pint (U.S. 1 cup) sour cream (more if
   desired)

FOR GARNISH

3 hard-boiled eggs, sliced

Cook the chopped parsley and sorrel leaves in the
soup stock for about 45 minutes. Add the lemon
juice, sugar, celery salt, salt and pepper. Remove
from the heat. When cold, stir in the sour cream.
Serve chilled with a garnish of sliced hard-boiled
eggs.

Schav is usually served on Shavuot and as a
refresher for summer meals.

Sorrel summer soup

FLEISHIDIKIR BORSHT

MEAT CABBAGE-BEETROOT SOUP

Cooking time   1½ hours
To serve   10—12

You will need

1 lb. stewing beef
4 pints (U.S. 10 cups) water
1 lb. cabbage
3 beetroots
1 carrot
3 onions
scant ¼ pint (U.S. ½ cup) tomato paste or
   ketchup or 1¼ lb. chopped tomatoes
1 tablespoon salt
¼ teaspoon white pepper
¼ teaspoon celery salt
1 bay leaf
6 allspice seeds (optional)
juice 1 large lemon
2 tablespoons sugar

TO GARNISH

8 boiled potatoes

Cut the stewing beef into cubes, shred the cabbage and grate the beetroots.
Slice the onions and chop the tomatoes, if you are using fresh ones.
Put the beef to cook in the water and when almost tender add the vegetables and simmer for about 30 minutes. Add tomato paste or tomatoes, seasonings and cook for a further 10 minutes, then add the

lemon juice and sugar and cook another 5 minutes. Use more lemon and sugar if you like a more pronounced seasoning. Serve hot with a boiled potato, cooked separately, for garnish.
This is the Jewish kosher adaptation of the Russian national soup.

MARAK YAYIN DUVDIVANIM

CHERRY WINE SOUP

Cooking time   30 minutes
To serve   6

You will need

1 lb. red cherries
3 whole cloves
1 small stick cinnamon
7 oz. sugar
2 pints (U.S. 5 cups) water
3 tablespoons cornflour
⅖ pint (U.S. 1 cup) red table wine
½ teaspoon grated lemon rind
lemon juice to taste
sour cream for garnish

Cook the cherries, cloves, cinnamon, sugar and water until the cherries are tender. Remove the spices. Dissolve the cornflour in the wine, add the lemon rind and juice and stir into the cherry liquid. Cook until clear. Serve chilled with a topping of sour cream.

Cherry wine soup

KRUPNIK

BARLEY-MUSHROOM SOUP

Cooking time 2¾ hours
To serve 10

You will need

2 tablespoons haricot beans (U.S. navy beans)
3¼ oz. pearl barley
8 oz. celery root, diced
2 parsnip roots, diced
2 carrots, diced
3 onions, diced
10 dried mushrooms
1 calf's foot
1 lb. brisket of beef
4⅘ pints (U.S. 12 cups) water
1 tablespoon salt
1 bay leaf
¼ teaspoon pepper
2 tablespoons oil

Rinse the beans and barley. Dice all the vegetables. Cook the beans, barley, calf's foot and beef for about 2½ hours, beginning with a medium heat and then low to simmer after the first 30 minutes. When meat is almost done add remaining ingredients except the onions and oil. Cook until meat and vegetables are done. Add more water if soup boils down too much. Remove the meat and calf's foot, and serve them separately. Fry the onions until golden in the oil, and add them to the soup. Cook a further 5 minutes and serve hot.

Note

This soup is so thick and filling that it is the main course of a dinner.

This soup born of poverty among the Jews of Poland, has become enriched in modern prosperous cookery with the addition of meat.

MARAK AVOCADO

AVOCADO SOUP

Cooking time about 2 minutes
To serve 8

You will need

5⅘ pints (U.S. 6 cups) hot chicken broth
1 lb. avocado pears, diced
salt and pepper to taste
⅖ pint (U.S. 1 cup) dry white wine
juice ½ lemon

FOR GARNISH

lemon slices

Put the hot broth, avocado pears and seasoning in the blender until smooth. Add the hot wine and lemon juice and heat, but do not boil, stirring well. Serve with a lemon slice.

This South American dish has become very Israeli.

Barley-mushroom soup

Avocado soup

FARFEL

DOUGH GRAINS

Cooking time   15 — 20 minutes
To serve   8

You will need

10 oz. flour
2 eggs
1 tablespoon cold water
½ teaspoon salt

FOR ROASTING

6 onions, diced finely
4 oz. chicken fat
10 oz. dried farfel (above)
1½ pints (U.S. 4 cups) soup or water
2 teaspoons salt
dash pepper

TO MAKE THE FARFEL

Mix the flour with the eggs, salt and water and knead well. Form into a ball and let it dry for 30 minutes if a dry warm day, and longer if a wet day. Grate coarsely and then spread out on a towel to dry thoroughly. This keeps for months, and is used as a garnish by boiling in soup.

FOR ROASTING THE FARFEL FOR A SIDE DISH TO MEAT

Fry the onions in the chicken fat on a low heat. Add the farfel and fry lightly. When golden, pour on the soup or water and cook until farfel swells to double its size. Add salt and pepper towards the end of cooking.
Farfel have been used as a soup garnish, or roasted for a side dish in Polish-Jewish kitchens for over five hundred years.

TRIFLACH

EGG DROPS FOR SOUP

Cooking time 5 minutes
To serve   8 — 10

You will need

2 eggs
6 tablespoons flour
scant ¼ pint (U.S. ½ cup) water
pinch salt

Beat the eggs. Add the flour, water and salt and mix well.
Gradually drop this mixture from end of spoon into boiling soup.
Cook 5 minutes until egg drops float to the top. These are light and fluffy.

BALLETJES
AND MERGBALLETJES

MEAT OR MARROW SOUP DUMPLINGS

Cooking time   15 — 20 minutes
To serve   8

You will need
Balletjes
6 oz. chopped beef
1 egg yolk
salt
pinch nutmeg

Mergballetjes
4 oz. raw beef marrow
2 eggs
1 tablespoon flour
salt
pinch nutmeg
2 slices white bread
water
dry breadcrumbs

TO MAKE THE BALLETJES

Mix all the ingredients and roll into tiny balls and boil in the soup.

TO MAKE THE MERGBALLETJES

In a thick pan melt the beef marrow over a low heat. Remove from the heat and leave to cool.
Beat the raw beef marrow with the eggs.
Add the flour, the salt and the nutmeg.
Dip the bread in the water and squeeze dry, then break the bread up and add to the marrow mixture.
Add enough breadcrumbs to make a stiff dough.
Roll into very small balls and boil in the soup.

A Dutch-Jewish dumpling for every festive chicken soup.

GILDERNEH YOICH
GOLDEN CHICKEN SOUP

Cooking time   1½ hours
To serve   8

You will need

1 boiling chicken
1 tablespoon salt
dash white pepper
4⅘ (U.S. 12 cups) water
3 carrots
3 onions
1 celery root or 6 stalks and leaves
2 parsnips
1 summer squash or 1 zucchini or
    1 small vegetable marrow

FOR GARNISH

lokshen (see page 22) *or* mandlen (see page 21)
or kreplach (see page 42) *or* matzo meal
knaidlach (see page 147) *or* farfel (see page 25)
or mergballetjes (see page 25) *or* balletjes (see
page 25) *or* rice

Cut up the chicken, season with salt and pepper
and then put to boil with remaining ingredients. If
some of the vegetables are out of season, more of the
others may be used. Cook on a low heat until the
chicken is very soft and the vegetables very well
done. Strain the soup and serve with any of the
above garnishes.
Gilderneh yoich is the traditional Friday night and
festival soup.

SMETENEH BORSHT
SOUR CREAM BEETROOT SOUP

(Illustrated in colour on page 20)
Cooking time   45 minutes
To serve   10 — 12

You will need

6 large beetroots
1 clove garlic
8 oz. celery root or stalks
1 large onion
2 tomatoes (optional)
4 pints (U.S. 10 cups) water
2 tablespoons vinegar
2 teaspoons salt
3 tablespoons sugar
4 tablespoons lemon juice
3 egg yolks
generous ½ pint (U.S. 1½ cups) sour cream

TO GARNISH

sliced cucumbers (optional)

Grate the beetroots, garlic, celery root, onion and
tomatoes if used. Add the water, vinegar and salt
and cook until vegetables are very soft. Strain the
soup for a light mixture, or put part through
a blender for a more bodied borsht. Add sugar and
lemon juice, and the beaten yolks, while the soup
is still hot. Do not boil. Cool and stir in the sour
cream. Serve chilled with a garnish of fresh
cucumber slices if desired.
Smeteneh borsht is an East-European summer soup
now on Jewish menus the world over.

Golden chicken soup with meat dumplings

DUMPLINGS AND NOODLES

KOOFTAHOT V'ITRIOT

It was not so long ago when Jewish mothers made their own lokshen — that is, noodles — at home, rolling out sheet after sheet of dough that was draped to dry on white cloths covering tables and chairs, and sofas and beds all over the house. The dough was then folded and the noodles cut to the desired width before final drying and storing. A supply for months was in my mother's cupboard, and all the brood and guests enjoyed every soup garnish and dessert that came out of it.

The same dough was made fresh often during the week, and while still moist and pliable was used for varenikis and varenitchkis. These names used to confuse our Gentile friends until they learned that varenitchkis were unfilled dough envelopes cooked up alone or with other things, while varenikis were pockets stuffed with cheese or fruits or meats, and that these also had another name — kreplach! But one thing they did know — that the dumplings were delicious.

Knishes are filled baked dumplings, served not only at meals, but in miniature size at parties. In Israel the similar Oriental borekas are served on the same occasions and are enjoyed as avidly by Western Jews as Eastern Jews who lay claim to their creation. Borekas come in various fillings, such as salty cheese or spinach or meat. Their doughs vary too: sometimes a flaky pastry is used, often a strudel thin dough is the thing, while short doughs and yeast doughs as well as noodle doughs are also acceptable. Knish or boreka . . . they belong to the great family of dumplings brought together in the Holy Land.

KUBEH

CRACKED WHEAT FILLED DUMPLINGS

Cooking time 20 minutes
To serve 6

You will need

2½ oz. burghul — finely cracked wheat
flour, if needed
1 onion, chopped
4 tablespoons oil
8 oz. minced lamb
3 tablespoons pine nuts and/or raisins
dash allspice
salt and pepper to taste

Soak the finely cracked wheat in water for at least 1 hour. Drain and pound in a mortar or put through the blender. Add flour if needed to hold the burghul together. Make a dumpling-size ball, insert a finger and work the wheat around to make a jacket. Fry the chopped onion in the oil, add the minced lamb and fry until the meat is no longer red. Add the pine nuts, or raisins, allspice, salt and pepper and mix thoroughly. Pack the filling into each dumpling and then close them. Flatten a little. Cook in boiling soup for about 20 minutes.

When boiled, kubeh is the Iraqi favourite dumpling with soups, and when fried it is a main dish.

VARIATION

Instead of boiling fry in very hot fat as a turnover.

Cracked wheat filled dumplings

KNISHES MIT NESHOMES

PASTIES WITH SOULS

Cooking time   30 minutes
To make   20 pasties

You will need

FLAKY PASTRY

8 oz. margarine
12 oz. flour, sifted
⅖ pint (U.S. 1 cup) boiling water
4 tablespoons oil

FILLING

8 oz. meat or liver or lung, or combined
salt and pepper
1 egg
20 small cracklings (see page 16)

TOPPING

1 egg yolk
1 teaspoon water
6 tablespoons sesame seeds

TO MAKE THE PASTRY

Mix the margarine with the sifted flour and add
the boiling water. Work into a dough and refrigerate overnight. Next day roll until very thin, then
spread with the oil and cut into 20 squares.

TO MAKE THE FILLING

Chop the meat or liver or lung. Chop and fry the
onion. Grind the meat and fried onion and add salt,

pepper and egg. Put a spoonful of this filling on
each square of pastry and put a crackling in the
middle.
Pinch edges together and seal into a ball. Turn over
the ball and pit it down a little.

TO GLAZE TOP

Brush the tops with egg yolk diluted with the water
and sprinkle with sesame seeds.
Bake in a moderate oven (350°F. or Gas Mark 4)
for about 30 minutes. Serve hot or warm.

Pasties with souls are an accompaniment to a main
dish or they can be served as a snack.

An olde-tyme Jewish dish with the crackling for
the soul.

RUOTA DI FARAONE

NOODLE SALAMI CASSEROLE

Cooking time   30 minutes
To serve   6

You will need

8 oz. narrow egg noodles
8 oz. salami
⅘ pint (U.S. 2 cups) meat sauce
   or soup
3¼ oz. raisins
5 oz. pine nuts or slivered almonds

Boil and drain the egg noodles. Slice the salami.
In a circular greased casserole put alternate layers
of noodles, meat sauce, sliced salami and a sprinkling of nuts and raisins.
The top layer should be of noodles with a circular
edging of salami.
Heat for about 20 minutes in a moderately hot oven
(400°F. or Gas Mark 6) then serve.

This Italian-Jewish dish is symbolic of the wheel
of Pharaoh's fate.

KASHA VARENITCHKES
NOODLES AND GROATS

Cooking time   30 minutes
To serve   6

You will need

THE DOUGH *

8 oz. flour
2 eggs
½ teaspoon salt
2 tablespoons water

THE KASHA

5⅓ oz. diced onions
3 oz. chicken fat
4 oz. buckwheat groats
about generous 1½ pints (U.S. 4 cups)
   boiling water
1 teaspoon salt
pinch pepper

* You can use wide egg noodles instead of the
dough for this dish.

Sift flour and make a well in the centre. Pour in
the eggs, salt and water, mix and knead well. Roll
out on floured board. Cut into 1½-inch squares and,
if you wish, pinch 2 of the corners together as in the
illustration, and let the dough dry somewhat while
you make the kasha.

Noodles and groats

Put the groats in a moderate oven (350°F. or Gas
Mark 4) for about 20 minutes, until a toast-like
brown. Fry the onions in the chicken fat. Add to the
groats and stir. Add boiling water to cover and return to the oven until groats have doubled in size
and the water absorbed. Stir in salt and pepper.
Keep warm and meanwhile cook the dough squares
in boiling salted water. When cooked mix with the
kasha and serve hot as an accompaniment to meat.

MAYEHREN TZIMMIS
MIT KNAIDLE
SWEET CARROTS
WITH DUMPLING

Cooking time   1½ hours
To serve   6—8

You will need

THE VEGETABLE

2 lb. carrots, sliced
water to cover
2 tablespoons chicken soup powder
3½ oz. sugar
salt and pepper
3 tablespoons flour
2 oz. chicken fat

THE DUMPLING

8 oz. self-raising flour
8 oz. chicken suet or margarine *
salt, pepper
scant ¼ pint (U.S. ½ cup) water
dash allspice or nutmeg

* suet is best for this dish

Cook carrots with water and soup powder for about
10 minutes. Add the sugar, salt and pepper and stir.
Make a cavity in the centre and put in the dumpling,
made by mixing all ingredients together. Continue
cooking for about 1 hour, adding a little water if
necessary, to keep the carrots immersed. Brown the
flour, add the chicken fat and stir. Pour about
⅔ pint (U.S. 1 cup) of the carrot stock on this
roux and stir over low heat until thick. Add the
mixture to the saucepan and cook for another
5 minutes.
This traditional dish is often made with a joint
of fat meat, or a chicken, in the saucepan.

FARFEL KUGEL
SWEET BAKED DOUGH GRAINS

Cooking time 30—40 minutes
To serve 6

You will need

10 oz. farfel (see page 25)
1 lb. or more fresh fruit *
4 eggs
7 oz. sugar (more if fruit is sour)
1 teaspoon vanilla essence
4 oz. butter or margarine

* Use any fruits in season that bake succulently, such as apples, peaches, cherries, loquats, quinces, plums or stewed dried fruits.

Cook the farfel in 1½ pints (U.S. 4 cups) boiling water with ½ teaspoon salt until almost double in bulk, drain and then rinse it in a sieve under a hot tap. Wash and slice the fruit and mix it with the farfel. Beat the eggs and sugar, add the vanilla essence and melted margarine. Add to the farfel, mix well and bake in a well-buttered casserole in a moderate oven (350°F. or Gas Mark 4) until golden on top.

Note

If you are using stewed dried fruits you will need less than 1 lb. and perhaps less sugar, depending on the fruit. The kugel must come out fruity and rather light.

Sweet baked dough grains

LEBER KNISHES
LIVER PASTIES

Cooking time 35 minutes
To make 15 pasties

You will need

PASTRY

8 oz. flour, self-raising
pinch salt
2 eggs
scant ¼ pint (U.S. ½ cup) oil
2 tablespoons water

FILLING

2 onions, chopped
6 tablespoons margarine
8 oz. chicken or other liver
salt and pepper
½ slice dry bread

GLAZING

1 egg yolk
1 teaspoon water

TO MAKE THE PASTRY

Sift dry ingredients together and form a mound. Make a well in centre and put in the eggs, oil and water and mix. Mix and knead. Roll out thinly and cut into squares or rounds.

TO MAKE THE FILLING

Fry the onions in half the margarine and remove. Then brown the lightly grilled livers in remaining margarine. Add the seasoning and put the mixture through the mincer together with the bread. Put a spoonful of filling on each round of pastry, bring and pinch edges together in the middle.

TO GLAZE

Brush top with egg diluted with the water and bake in a well-greased pan for about 35 minutes until golden in a moderate oven (350°F. or Gas Mark 4). An accompaniment to a main dish or served as a snack.

VARIATION

Mushrooms may be added to the onions during frying.

SHABBES GANEF KNAIDL
SABBATH THIEF DUMPLING

Cooking time   at least 1 hour
To serve   6

You will need

4 oz. self-raising flour
1½ oz. semolina
½ teaspoon salt
dash pepper
1 egg, beaten
4 tablespoons water
4 oz. margarine, diced
pinch nutmeg

Mix all ingredients together and put the dumpling
(or you can divide this into six small dumplings)
into the pot with a pot roast, cholent, tzimmis or
kishke, adding a little extra water to make a gravy
in which the knaidl will cook. Begin with high heat
and then reduce heat. Cook in a covered pot for
at least 1 hour. This can also cook overnight with
a cholent.

An accompaniment to a main dish.

SCHNITZEL-KLOESE
FRUIT DUMPLINGS

Cooking time   4 hours or more
To serve   8

You will need

8 oz. self-raising flour
8 oz. chopped suet or margarine
½ teaspoon salt
dash nutmeg
sugar
water
chicken fat
cut up dried fruits — prunes, pears, peaches,
apricots

Mix flour, suet or margarine, salt, nutmeg, 4 tablespoons sugar and scant ¼ pint (U.S. ½ cup) water
to make a dough.
Divide into 8 dumplings and fry in chicken fat to
brown all over.
Put into a casserole with the chicken fat and top

Fruit dumplings

with the cut-up dried fruits and if desired add extra
sugar to taste. Cover with water. Bring to the boil,
cover, and then put into a very cool oven (200°F.
or Gas Mark ¼) to gently cook overnight. Serve hot.
These dumplings can accompany a main dish or
be served as a dessert.

A German-Jewish dish that cooks all night in
preparation for the Sabbath.

SAUERKRAUT KNISHES
SAUERKRAUT PASTIES

Cooking time   30 minutes
To make   about 12 pasties

You will need

THE PASTRY

1 egg
scant ¼ pint (U.S. ½ cup) sour cream
1 oz. margarine, melted
½ teaspoon salt
6 oz. flour, sifted

FILLING

1 lb. sauerkraut
1 onion, diced
2 oz. butter
2 tablespoons brown sugar
pinch caraway seeds (optional)
milk for topping

TO MAKE THE PASTRY

Beat the egg, add sour cream, melted margarine, salt and flour. Roll out on a floured board and cut into circles.

TO MAKE THE FILLING

Rinse and drain the sauerkraut. Fry the onion in the butter until golden and then add the sauerkraut, and cook for about 20 minutes on a low flame. Add the sugar and cook until golden. Add caraway seeds if used.

When cool, put a heaped spoonful of filling on each circle, then fold over to form half-circles and pinch edges together. Brush tops with milk and bake in a greased pan in a moderately hot oven (375°F. or Gas Mark 5) until golden (about 30 minutes). These are an excellent accompaniment to a main dish or can be served as a snack.

Note

These are also known as pirogen. Sauerkraut Knishes are of Germanic-Jewish origin and became popular all through Central Europe.

PAPANUSH

SEMOLINA DUMPLINGS

Cooking time
To serve   6

You will need

⅘ pint (U.S. 2 cups) milk
6½ oz. semolina or cornmeal
2 oz. butter
½ teaspoon salt
2 tablespoons sugar
4 eggs, lightly beaten
8 oz. cottage cheese, sieved

FOR GARNISH

butter as desired
sour cream and honey, mixed

Bring the milk to the boil and slowly sprinkle in the semolina or cornmeal, stirring constantly. Add the butter, salt and sugar and cook until mixture is thick. Cool somewhat and then add the eggs and cheese. Shape into dumplings (if you wish, put a dent in each dumpling by pressing in your thumb). Boil in salted water for about 25 minutes. Drain. Serve hot with a piece of butter in each dent, and garnish with sour cream and honey to taste.
A Rumanian treat for Shavuot.

Semolina dumplings

KASHA PIROSHKI

BUCKWHEAT GROAT PASTIES

Cooking time   40 minutes
To serve   8

You will need

1 egg
4 oz. buckwheat groats
boiling water
4 large onions, diced
3 tablespoons oil
potato pastry (see page 34)
oil or egg for brushing

Beat the egg and mix with the buckwheat groats, then place in a slow oven (300°F. or Gas Mark 1—2) to dry. When dried, break up the egg and buckwheat mixture with a spoon and cover with boiling water.

Fry the onions in the oil and add to the dried groats. Place a spoonful of groats mixture in centre of each square of potato dough, bring corners together and seal all the edges. Brush with a little oil or diluted egg.

Bake edge-pinched side down in a greased pan in a moderate oven (350°F. or Gas Mark 4) until golden. This should take about 25 minutes.

Buckwheat groat pasties are an excellent accompaniment to a main dish. Alternatively they can be served as a snack.

Buckwheat groats is a much loved Jewish dish from the Baltic lands and Russia.

Potato pasties

KARTOFFEL KNISHES

POTATO PASTIES

Cooking time 20 minutes
To serve 8

You will need

POTATO PASTRY

7 large potatoes, boiled
2 eggs
½ oz. margarine, melted
salt to taste
self-raising flour as needed
1 tablespoon oil

FILLING

5⅓ oz. diced onions
2 oz. chicken fat
14 oz. mashed potatoes
2 eggs
1 teaspoon salt
⅛ teaspoon white pepper
dash celery salt (optional)

FOR THE PASTRY

Boil and mash the potatoes, beat in the eggs and margarine. Add salt to taste. Add enough flour to enable you to roll out the dough. Roll out to ¼ inch thickness. Cut into 16 squares and top each with a spoonful of the filling. Fold over into triangles or bring four corners to a point and seal to form balls. Brush with oil put in a greased pan and bake in a moderate oven (350°F. or Gas Mark 4) until golden (about 20 minutes).

34

TO MAKE THE FILLING

Fry the onions in the chicken fat and then add remaining ingredients and work to a smooth mixture. Potato pasties are served as hot tidbits at weddings, bar-mizvas and brith milah.

VARIATION

Any other pastry can be used instead of the potato dough.

KARTOFEL HALKES

FILLED POTATO DUMPLING

Cooking time 2 hours
To serve 4—6

You will need

THE DUMPLING

3 large raw potatoes
1 cooked potato
1 oz. chicken fat
1 tablespoon chopped onion
6 tablespoons matzo meal
3 eggs
salt and pepper
dash cinnamon

THE FILLING

8 oz. ground meat
1 onion, chopped
salt and pepper
dash cinnamon

TO MAKE THE DUMPLING

Finely grate the raw potatoes and drain well. Squeeze potatoes from time to time to expel liquid. Mash the cooked potato and add. Mix with remaining ingredients and set aside for 2 hours. Form into 1 or 2 large balls. Hollow out the balls.

TO MAKE THE FILLING

Mix all ingredients.
Put the filling inside the balls and seal. Cook the dumpling on a bed of raw carrots (as for tzimmis) or in gravy alongside the meat.

This is the Passover version of the tzimmis or cholent knaidl.

PIROSHKI
BAKED PASTIES

Cooking time   30 minutes
To make   32 pasties

You will need

DOUGH

1 oz. fresh yeast
1 tablespoon sugar
⅖ pint (U.S. 2 cups) lukewarm milk
1 lb. flour
4 eggs, lightly beaten
4 oz. butter or margarine, melted
¼ teaspoon salt

FILLING

2 lb. potatoes, cooked
2 onions
1½ oz. margarine
3 oz. grated yellow cheese
6 tablespoons cottage cheese

TOPPING

1 egg, diluted with milk

TO MAKE THE DOUGH

Dissolve the yeast with sugar and a little of the milk. Sift flour. Add the milk and yeast mixture and mix well. Leave to rise, covered with a cloth, in a warm place for 30 minutes. Then add remaining dough ingredients and knead until elastic. Leave to rise again until double in bulk. Roll the dough out to ¼ inch thickness and cut into circles.

TO MAKE THE FILLING

Mash the potatoes. Fry the onions in the margarine and mix with the potatoes and two cheeses. Put a tablespoon of the filling on each round of dough. Fold over to make half moons and pinch edges together. Brush with diluted egg yolk. Bake in a very moderate oven (350°F. or Gas Mark 4) for about 30 minutes, until piroshki are golden and done.

PURIM VARENIKIS
FEAST OF LOTS POCKETS

Cooking time   about 10 minutes
To serve   6—8

You will need

1 recipe kreplach dough (see page 42)
cherry, plum or strawberry jam
   (with fruit in it)
breadcrumbs (as required)

Cut the kreplach dough into small squares. Put a spoonful of jam and breadcrumb mixture in each. Use only enough breadcrumbs to keep jam from being runny. Fold over into triangles and pinch edges together. Bring two corners together to make a purse shape. Cook a few at a time in boiling slightly salted water. They are cooked when they rise to the top. Serve with butter or sugar or sour cream or stewed cherries or strawberries or plums. Varenikis are kreplach, which are boiled pierogi — Jewish raviolis.

BOREKAS

BAKED SPINACH TURNOVERS

(Illustrated in colour on opposite page)

Cooking time   25 minutes
To make   20 turnovers

You will need

DOUGH

8 oz. margarine or butter
1 teaspoon salt
12 oz. self-raising flour
lukewarm water

FILLING

2 oz. grated yellow cheese
6½ oz. cooked spinach
3 egg yolks

FINISHING

1 egg yolk
1 teaspoon water
sesame seeds

TO MAKE THE DOUGH

Melt the margarine and rub into the flour and salt.
Add enough water to be able to roll the dough.
Roll out and cut into small rounds.

TO MAKE THE FILLING

Mix all the ingredients and put a heaped spoonful
on each round. Fold dough over in two and pinch
the edges together.

TO FINISH

Dilute egg yolk with the water and brush each
pastry. Then sprinkle on a few sesame seeds. Bake
in a buttered pan until golden for about 25 minutes
in a moderately hot oven (375°F. or Gas Mark 6).

VARIATIONS

Different doughs may be used such as flaky pastry,
paper-thin strudel dough or rich noodle dough.

Fillings can be of Katzkaval cheese or any other
yellow cheese with spinach. Sometimes they are
made with cottage cheese and spinach or white and
yellow cheeses mixed without spinach. Meat and
spinach, or meat without spinach, are also popular.
Sometimes, with flaky pastry, the dough is cut into
squares, filled and folded over without sealing.
Sometimes the borekas are round and bun-shaped.

MILINA

NOODLE CHICKEN-BRAIN BAKE

Cooking time   45 minutes
To serve   6—8

You will need

2 large onions, chopped
4 tablespoons oil
2 tablespoons parsley, chopped
1 calf's brain, cooked
1 chicken's breast, cooked
8 oz. broad noodles, boiled
2 hard-boiled eggs, diced
6 raw eggs
salt and pepper
dash allspice

Fry the onions in the oil until golden, then add the
parsley. Dice the brain and breasts and add. In
a well greased casserole put alternate layers of
broad noodles, meat mixture and diced eggs, and
finish with noodles on top. Beat raw eggs, add
seasoning and pour on the mixture. Bake for about
45 minutes in a very cool oven (275°F. or Gas
Mark ½—1).

Note

Traditionally this is made with sheets of noodle
dough (see page 128) instead of broad noodles.

Baked spinach turnovers

Four kinds of cottage cheese spread

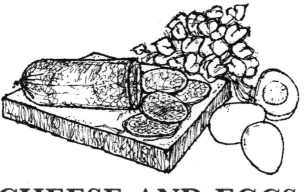

CHEESE AND EGGS

MA'ACHALEI BETZIM V'GVINOT

Cheese dishes seem to have a very long history in Jewish cooking. The Bible tells of David being offered a variety of cow's cheeses at Mahanaim. It seemed to be a favourite family dish, for King David's father, Jesse, also gave a gift of ten slices of cheese (referred to as milk, undoubtedly curdled) to an officer in charge of his sons.

Cottage cheeses and salted white pressed cheese — of cows, sheep and goats — are the most used cheeses in Jewish communities everywhere, going into such dishes as kreplach and strudels and borekas and spreads and cakes.

The cured yellow cheeses have been introduced into Jewish cuisine only in recent years, for they were not considered kosher due to the curdling ingredient taken from the stomach lining of stock. One of the most popular egg dishes among Oriental Jews is the hamindas. These eggs are cooked in shell for many hours, until they get nutty brown all through, with an unusual velvety texture and mellow flavour. Because of the required long cooking these eggs are often served on the Sabbath along with hamim (see page 71) simmering together in the same saucepan overnight, and served hot at table after the Synagogue services.

Salami with eggs is as popular among Western Jews as bacon and eggs is with Gentiles. As the two are apparently not so far different in taste, the dish is evidence of similar tastes among different peoples.

ESSER HARITZEH GVINA

TEN KINDS OF COTTAGE CHEESE SPREADS

(Illustrated in colour on opposite page and in black and white on page 43)

No cooking

You will need

8 oz. cottage cheese
scant ¼ pint (U.S. ½ cup) sour cream
salt to taste

Mix all the above together and then add any of the following to the desired taste and colour. Grate, chop, grind ingredients opposite or put through a blender.

GREEN parsley or celery tops or onion tops or green peppers or raw spinach

PEACH smoked salmon or lox

YELLOW curry powder or turmeric or egg yolks or a combination

PINK-ROSE paprika or pimento peppers

MUSTARD mustard

BROWN black olives or anchovies

WHITE celery root or onion

MAUVE-CYCLAMEN beetroot, raw or cooked

ALMOND GREEN avocado

FLECKED slivers of pimento, green pepper, carrot, caraway seed, chopped onion top (do not put this through the blender)

Cottage cheese strudel

KAESE STRUDEL
COTTAGE CHEESE STRUDEL

Cooking time   25 minutes
To serve   6—8

You will need

1 recipe strudel dough (see below)
2 oz. butter, melted
1½ lb. cottage cheese
2 tablespoons semolina
2 eggs
3 tablespoons sugar
1 teaspoon salt
1 teaspoon vanilla
3 oz. raisins (optional)

FOR TOPPING

sprinkling icing sugar *or*
⅖ pint (U.S. 1 cup) sour cream
honey or sugar, if desired

STRUDEL DOUGH

10 oz. flour
1 teaspoon salt
2 tablespoons oil
2 eggs
¼ pint (U.S. ⅔ cup) lukewarm water

TO MAKE THE STRUDEL DOUGH

See apple strudel (page 128). Sprinkled melted butter on the strudel dough. Mix the cottage cheese, semolina, eggs, sugar, salt, vanilla and raisins. Put the cheese mixture along one edge of the dough and roll up. Put into a buttered pan, cut into serving pieces. Bake for about 25 minutes in a moderate oven (350°F. or Gas Mark 4) until golden. Serve hot with a topping of icing sugar or sour cream to which honey or sugar may be added. This Austrian-Jewish dish is called 'kizi-knish' in other communities. This dish is also good cold.

HAMINDAS
BAKED BROWN EGGS

Cooking time   12 hours or more
To serve   6

You will need

12 eggs
cold water to cover
2 tablespoons oil
1 large onion, with peel
pinch pepper

Cover the eggs with the water, add oil, onion and pepper. Bake in a casserole covered with brown wrapping paper in a very cool oven (200°F. or Gas Mark 0) for about 12 hours or more. Serve hot or cold.
An ancient Sephardic dish for Sabbath brunch.

Note

Eggs are sometimes baked or simmered overnight with the hamim (see page 71) with much the same result.

Baked brown eggs

Spinach cheese bake

Salami omelet

SPONGHUS
SPINACH CHEESE BAKE

Cooking time   30 minutes
To serve   6

You will need

2 lb. spinach, washed and chopped
1 teaspoon salt
¾ oz. chopped parsley
6 tablespoons oil
6 eggs, lightly beaten
½ teaspoon black pepper
8 oz. salt goat's cheese, finely grated

Mix spinach with salt. Let drip 5 minutes. Add chopped parsley. Pour on oil and spread in shallow baking pan. Mix eggs, pepper and cheese. Make 6 hollows in spinach and put cheese mixture into each. Bake in a moderately hot (400°F. or Gas Mark 6) oven for 30 minutes.

KOHLBUHS MIT AYER
SALAMI OMELET

Cooking time   3 minutes
To serve   6

You will need

6 eggs
6 tablespoons water
salt and pepper to taste
2 tablespoons oil

18 slices salami *

* Any type of salami or smoked meat can be used in this dish.

Lightly beat the eggs, add the water, salt and pepper. Heat the oil in a frying pan, add the salami slices. Turn the salami when the pieces just begin to brown. Pour on the egg mixture and fry until the eggs set. If you wish you can turn over the omelet, fry for about ½ minute and serve at once.
From the kitchens of Central and Eastern European Jews.

SAMBOUSEK
FRIED YEAST TURNOVERS

Cooking time   3 minutes

You will need

1 recipe yeast dough (see gugelhupf, page 127)
melted margarine
12 oz. cottage cheese
4 oz. goat cheese or katzkaval, grated
1 egg
salt to taste
fat for frying

Roll dough out thinly before it has been put to rise. Sprinkle with melted margarine. Cut into large rounds. Mix remaining ingredients and put a spoonful on each round. Fold over and pinch edges together. Set aside for 30 minutes, covered, to rise and then fry in deep hot fat.
A Near Eastern favourite on Shavuot.

SHAVUOT KREPLACH

PENTECOST CHEESE POCKETS

Cooking time 15 minutes
To make 18 kreplach

You will need

DOUGH

1 lb. flour, sifted
2 eggs
⅖ pint (U.S. 1 cup) lukewarm water

FILLING

1 lb. cottage cheese
2 egg yolks
1 oz. margarine
2 tablespoons sugar
¼ teaspoon salt
3 tablespoons raisins (optional)

TOPPING

sour cream
sugar

For the dough mix flour, eggs and enough luke-warm water to make a soft mixture. Roll out thinly on a floured board and cut into squares.
Mix all filling ingredients and put a spoonful on each square. Fold over and press together, then bring two corners together to form a little purse. Cook in boiling water. When the kreplach float to the top remove and serve them with a topping of sour cream and sugar.
Cottage cheese dishes are traditionally eaten on the festival of Shavuot.

VARIATION

For a more savoury type of kreplach these can be made without sugar, or margarine, or raisins, but instead 3 tablespoons of sour cream are added to the cottage cheese.

KALSOHNEHS

CHEESE TURNOVERS

Cooking time 18 minutes
To make 15 kalsohnehs

You will need

THE DOUGH

6 oz. flour
pinch salt
2 eggs

THE FILLING

12 oz. salt white goat cheese
4 tablespoons sour cream
2 eggs
butter for frying

Mix all the dough ingredients together and thinly roll out. Cut into 2-inch squares and top with the filling prepared by mashing the cheese and working in remaining ingredients. Fold over the dough and press edges together in the shape of triangular pockets. Boil in lightly salted water and then fry in butter. Serve hot with yoghourt or sour cream.

A Balkan-Jewish dish of the Shavuot festival.

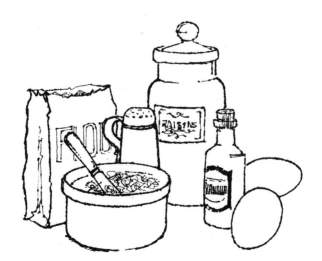

Six kinds of cottage cheese spread

CEREALS

MA'ACHALEI DAGAN

In Jewish cooking cereals are more of a main dish than a breakfast food, but grains run the gamut of every course. Though cereals — like bread — are the main bulk food of the non-affluent masses everywhere, prosperity has not been able to wean the palate of their use even in *haute cuisine*. But the most basic grains have been glamourised to make some of the finest food imaginable. In Jewish cooking it holds a prime place.

Burghul — cracked wheat — is especially loved in Jewish cooking of the Middle East. Even in the Bible (Zechariah 9:17) it says that grain delighted young men, just as wine overwhelmed women, and so the food has a long culinary tradition. It goes into the making of many dishes from main accompaniments to dumplings or puddings, from the savoury to the sweet.

Rice is not limited to the Far Eastern kitchen where it is served in huge heaps. One can have a gourmet Bokharian pilaff as colourful as the striped cloak and embroidered skullcap of one's Sabbath host, or a mejedrah from an Iraqi Jewish table or a tzimmis of rice and fruits that came from the Jewish kitchens of Central Europe, which are no more.

Chick peas and barley and beans go into many of the Sabbath cholents. In all the recipes the overnight simmering improves the flavour and enables the housewife to serve warm food without preparing it on the Day of Rest. Other grains such as buckwheat groats go into the making of much-loved kashas inspired by Russian and Polish cooking, and cornmeal is a favourite of Rumanians.

BURGHUL
CRACKED WHEAT

Cooking time 2 hours 15 minutes
To serve 6

You will need

12 oz. burghul (cracked wheat)
1 clove garlic, crushed
6 tablespoons oil
1¼ pints (U.S. 3 cups) soup stock
salt, pepper and cayenne

* Burghul is used in many Near Eastern dishes, and can be purchased in speciality shops offering Mediterranean ingredients.

Lightly fry the burghul and garlic in the oil. Add the stock and simmer for about 2 hours — until stock is all absorbed. Add salt, pepper and cayenne to suit your taste.

Burghul is on the board of every Jewish home of the Middle East.

MAMALIGI
CORN MEAL PORRIDGE

Cooking time 40 minutes
To serve 6

You will need

generous 1½ pints (U.S. 4 cups) boiling water
1 teaspoon salt
11 oz. corn meal
3 oz. butter or margarine

To the boiling water add the salt and with a wooden spoon slowly stir in the corn meal. Cook, stirring continuously, until thick. Add the butter or margarine, reduce heat and let corn meal cook 30 min-

Corn meal porridge

Fruited rice with meat

utes more. When the mamaligi no longer sticks to the pan, turn it out on a platter or board. Serve warm with butter, or chicken fat, gravy or grated Katzkaval cheese. It can also be a side dish to meat.

Note

When ¼ oz. fresh yeast, 4 oz. flour, ¼ pint (U.S. ⅝ cup) milk, 2 eggs and 2 tablespoons sugar are added to above recipe after cooking cornmeal mixture, and the mixture is shaped into pancakes and baked for 15 minutes, it is called Malai.

RIEZ TZIMMIS

FRUITED RICE WITH MEAT

Cooking time   3 hours
To serve   6

You will need

3¼ oz. dried prunes and/or apricots
2 lb. brisket of beef
4 tablespoons oil
2 teaspoons salt
water
7 oz. rice
rind and juice ½ lemon
¼ teaspoon cinnamon
⅛ teaspoon nutmeg

Soak the prunes and/or apricots for 2 hours. Brown the beef in the oil. Add salt and a little water to pot roast the meat over a medium heat until almost done (about 2½ hours). Add the rice, fruit and seasonings. Cover with boiling water and cook over

a low heat for 20—30 minutes more, until rice and fruit are done.

CHOLENT

SABBATH OVERNIGHT STEW

Cooking time   10—12 hours
To serve   6

You will need

1½ oz. fat
1 lb. beef brisket or chopped beef
8 oz. dried beans or chick peas, soaked
   overnight
4 onions, diced
1 clove garlic, chopped
6 tablespoons pearl barley
8 medium-sized potatoes, halved
salt and pepper to taste
water
shabbes ganef knaidl (optional) (see page 32)
Heat the fat and sear the meat. If using chopped beef roll into a ball. Put all the ingredients in a large heavy saucepan. Cover with boiling water and bring to the boil. Set over a very low heat or in a very slow oven (225°F. or Gas Mark 0) and cook, covered, overnight. Do not stir up cholent, but shake the saucepan and add water if needed.

This dish is recorded in Italy five hundred years ago and now is an international Jewish dish. This original barley bean cholent can be called shalet, sholet, sholend or chunt.

MEJEDRAH
PILAFF OF LENTILS AND RICE

(Illustrated in colour on opposite page)

Cooking time　2 hours
To serve　　　6

You will need

3 large onions, sliced
3 tablespoons olive oil
3 tablespoons pine nuts
　or slivered almonds
8 oz. whole brown lentils *
soup stock
8 oz. long grain rice
salt and pepper

* Lentils must be of the whole brown variety, so
　they retain their shape.

Fry the sliced onions in the olive oil until golden
and crisp, then add the pine nuts and fry until just
golden.
Remove and put them aside for the garnish.
Put the lentils in the oil, cover with soup stock
and simmer for about 1½ hours until lentils are
almost soft.
Add the rice and more stock, with salt and pepper
to taste. Bring to the boil and then reduce the heat
and cook for 15 minutes more. Moisture should be
absorbed.
Serve hot, topped with the fried onions and pine
nuts.
A Jewish Near Eastern dish served on most
festivals.

PILAU BOKHARI
BOKHARIAN PILAFF

(Illustrated in colour on opposite page)

Cooking time　45 minutes
To serve　　　6

You will need

10 chicken livers
3 oz. chicken fat
8 oz. coarsely grated carrots
2 onions, chopped
¾ oz. parsley, chopped
generous 1¾ pints (U.S. 4½ cups) water
　or stock
10½ oz. rice
1½ teaspoons turmeric
salt and pepper to taste
2 large tomatoes, diced
a little garlic or garlic salt added if you wish

Lightly grill the livers in the chicken fat and then
dice them. Lightly fry the carrots, onion and
parsley. Put all ingredients except the tomatoes
into a heavy covered saucepan and cook without
stirring for about 30 minutes. Add the diced
tomatoes and heat through.
This dish is as colourful as the robes of the Bokharian
Jews.

VARIATIONS

The turmeric can be omitted. The vegetables, rice
and livers cubes can be layered to form a different
pattern.

Pilaff of lentils and rice; Bokharian pilaff

Raw potato pancakes

PANCAKES AND BLINTZES

LEVIVOT V'BLINTZES

One of the most longed-for dishes among assimilated Jews is blintzes — 'the treat that Mamma used to make'. As a result, these crêpes have proved one of the chief attractions of kosher restaurants in the Western world, where suburbanites take their families for supper on a Sunday night. Because of its cheese filling — a traditional food of Shavuot — millions of blintzes are made in Israel on this festival. In the United States two blintzes are placed on a plate to look like Scrolls to commemorate the receiving of the Torah on this occasion at Mount Sinai. The usual topping is sour cream with jam or stewed berries. As strawberries are at the height of harvest in Israel during Shavuot, this fruit and whipped cream are quickly gaining favour as a topping for blintzes.

Pancakes are the traditional treat of the Hanuka festival. They are fried in oil to commemorate the oil found by the Maccabeans when they recaptured Jerusalem from the Syrians two thousand years ago. The one day's supply of oil burned for a week. Therefore the festival is celebrated for eight days and the pancake-latkes can be garnished in different ways all week, varying from apple sauce to sour cream, or sugar and cinnamon, or taken with cracklings, or even served in gravy as a side dish to meat or poultry.

Though pancakes of all lands have an appreciated place on Jewish menus, neither the French crêpe-suzette nor the American flapjack have been able to take over the popularity of either the blintzes or the latkes.

MATZOPLETZEL

MATZO PANCAKES

Cooking time   about 3 minutes
To serve   6

You will need

1⅕ pints (U.S. 3 cups) boiling water
6 matzos
6 eggs
1½ teaspoons salt
fat for frying

TOPPING

sugar and cinnamon to taste or
sour cream mixed with honey or jam

Pour the boiling water over the matzos and set aside for 10 minutes. Squeeze out the liquid and then mash the matzos. Add the eggs and salt and mix well. Drop the mixture by spoonfuls into hot fat and fry until golden on both sides. Serve at once with a topping of sugar and cinnamon or sour cream mixed with honey or jam to taste.

This is an excellent dish for breakfast or for supper.

Matzo pancakes can also be served as a dessert.

Note

To make a savoury matzo pancake, add a dash of pepper and a dash of onion salt but omit the topping of sugar and cinnamon or sour cream mixed with honey.

Cottage cheese crêpes

BLINTZES
COTTAGE CHEESE CRÊPES

Cooking time 2—3 minutes
To serve 8

You will need

THE BATTER

2 medium-sized eggs
generous ¼ pint (U.S. ¾ cup) milk
1 oz. margarine, melted
¼ teaspoon salt
2 oz. flour, sifted

THE FILLING

1 lb. cottage cheese
2 tablespoons sour cream
2 egg yolks
3 tablespoons sugar
1 teaspoon vanilla essence
½ teaspoon salt
raisins are sometimes added to the filling

FOR TOPPING (optional)

sour cream *or* whipped cream *or* stewed berries
or honey *or* any of these combined.

TO MAKE THE BATTER

Lightly beat the eggs and milk together then add
the melted margarine, salt and sifted flour. Lightly
grease a small pan and spoon in a little batter,
tilting the pan to spread it thinly and evenly. Cook

over medium heat until the batter just sets, then
turn out, bottom side up, on to a cloth.

TO MAKE THE FILLING

Mix all the ingredients and spread over the crêpes.
Fold over into fan shapes or roll up. Brown the
blintzes in butter just before serving.
Top with sour or whipped cream, or stewed
berries, or honey, or any of these combined. Also
served plain, if desired.
All Ashkenazic (Western) Jewish kitchens feature
this fine dish.

FRUTADAS
THREE-TONE VEGETABLE PANCAKES

Cooking time about 2 minutes
To serve 6

You will need

2½ oz. flour
3 eggs
3 teaspoons sugar
salt to taste
2½ oz. chopped cooked white leeks
2½ oz. chopped cooked green spinach
2½ oz. chopped cooked yellow pumpkin
  or carrots
cooking oil

Each pancake is of only one vegetable to have

Three-tone vegetable pancakes

variety of colour on the plate. Mix the flour, eggs, sugar and salt and divide among each batch of vegetables. Form into small patties and fry in the oil until only just cooked so pancakes do not brown too much.

Turkish Jews make this on Rosh Hashono in three colours to symbolize the variety of the harvest.

LABTAH

POTATO AND WALNUT PANCAKES

Cooking time 4—5 minutes
To serve 8

You will need

2 oz. chopped suet
2 tablespoons oil
2 lb. cooked potatoes
4 eggs
4 oz. walnuts, chopped
2 teaspoons salt
¼ teaspoon white pepper

TO GARNISH

walnuts
chopped lettuce

Melt the suet in a heavy pan. Add the oil and heat well. Mash the potatoes, and eggs, chopped walnuts and salt and pepper. Fry into one large

Potato and walnut pancakes

(traditional pattern) or 8 small pancakes, until crusted and golden on both sides. Garnish with walnuts and chopped lettuce. Serve hot.
A Georgian favourite for Passover or Hanuka.

LEBER-MAYINA

PANCAKE-LIVER BAKE

Cooking time 40 minutes
To serve 6

You will need

FILLING

12 oz. liver
2 onions, sliced
1 oz. chicken fat
2—3 cracklings (see page 16)
6 eggs, separated
dash nutmeg
salt and pepper
1½ oz. matzo meal

PANCAKES

3 eggs
2 tablespoons water
1 tablespoon potato starch
¼ teaspoon salt
fat for frying

Grill the liver beforehand until firm.
Fry the onions in the chicken fat and put both through the mincer together with the cracklings. Add the beaten egg yolks, nutmeg, salt, pepper, and just before cooking fold in the stiffly beaten egg whites alternately with the matzo meal.

TO MAKE THE PANCAKES

Mix together the eggs and water in which the potato starch and salt have been diluted. Grease a large frying pan and pour on one-third of the mixture at a time, tilting the pan to spread the pancake. Fry only one side and then put the pancake on a towel. After preparing the three pancakes, put one into a casserole and cover it with half the liver mixture. Put on the next pancake and add remaining liver mixture. Top with the third pancake. Bake for about 20 minutes in a very moderate oven (300°F. or Gas Mark 2) until top is golden.
'Mayina' is an adaptation from the Passover Turkish 'Minas'.

VARIATIONS

Cooked ground beef or fowl may be used with the liver, or by itself.

51

KARTOFFEL LATKES
RAW POTATO PANCAKES

(Illustrated in colour on page 48)
Cooking time   4 minutes
To serve   6

You will need

1 onion
6 medium-sized potatoes
½ teaspoon bicarbonate of soda
2 eggs
2 oz. flour
salt and pepper to taste
fat for frying

Finely grate the onion and then potatoes. Mix with the bicarbonate of soda. Drain off any liquid and beat in the remaining ingredients. Heat fat and when hot drop batter by tablespoons on to a pan. Fry until golden on the outside. Turn over only once. Serve with apple sauce or sour cream or sugar and cinnamon or greben cracklings. The traditional treat for the festival of Hanuka.

BEOLAS
TUNISIAN BEIGNETS

(Illustrated on opposite page)
Cooking time   2—3 minutes
To serve   6

You will need

2 tablespoons ground nuts (optional)
2 oz. matzo meal
6 eggs, well beaten
oil for frying
few drops orange essence
grated rind 1 orange
3 tablespoons honey

Mix the ground nuts, if used, with the matzo meal and the well-beaten eggs. Drop the mixture by spoonfuls into hot oil and fry until golden. Drain on paper. Add orange essence and/or grated orange rind to the honey.
Put each beignet on a toothpick and dip in the honey.

Though always served on Passover in Tunis, they also make a year-round treat as a beignet.

LEVIVOT HALAMIT
MALLOW PANCAKES

Cooking time   about 3 minutes
To serve   6

You will need

1 lb. chopped mallow (or other greens such as spinach)
2 tablespoons chopped parsley
4 oz. dry breadcrumbs
3 tablespoons flour
salt and pepper to taste
dash nutmeg
dash celery salt
3 eggs, lightly beaten
oil for frying

Wash the greens and cook with very little water until vegetable has wilted (about 5 minutes). Drain and add the parsley, breadcrumbs, salt, pepper, nutmeg, celery salt and stir in the beaten eggs. Drop the mixture from a tablespoon into hot fat. Fry until golden on both sides.

The wild crispa mallow related to the 'Jews-Mallow' kept Israelis from starving in Jerusalem during the siege of the city in 1948. It is now enhanced with other ingredients and served as a symbol on Independence Day.

Tunisian beignets

BREAD

LECHEM

Bread is more than the 'Staff of Life' in Jewish tradition. A pinch of the dough is symbolically cast into the fire in memory of the 'first portion' (the tax) given to the priests of the Temple in Old Testament days.

Those of us who lived through the Jerusalem siege of 1948, when the war of liberation was being fought in Palestine, know how good is the taste of any bread. For weeks we survived on four slices of black bread a day, supplemented from time to time with a few spoonfuls of beans or a little fat or powdered milk for babies. When the Israel Army broke through the Arab lines after the declaration of the State and brought us flour for white bread, it was more exciting than a wedding cake to a bride.

Today one can choose of this bread and that, and even have it ready sliced for the toaster.

Oh, the glory of our braided Sabbath loaves which we bless at table, thanking the Lord for drawing bread out of the soil! We could also have it all week but we cherish it for the Holy Day of Rest.

Instead we can indulge in sweet bilkes, savoury pampalik with a sprinkling of toasted onion, crusty bagels to eat with cream cheese and smoked salmon (popularly called lox), pita pancake bread of the Middle East, the hearty rye bread with a whiff of caraway seed, and many others.

CHALLA

SABBATH AND FESTIVAL BREAD

(Illustrated in colour on page 56)
Cooking time 1 hour
To make 2 loaves

You will need

3 tablespoons sugar
1 oz. dried yeast
1 pint (U.S. 2½ cups) warm water
2¼ lb. flour, sifted
3 teaspoons salt
3 eggs, lightly beaten
4 tablespoons oil

TO GLAZE

1 egg yolk
2 tablespoons water
poppy or sesame seeds for sprinkling

Mix sugar, yeast and scant ¼ pint (U.S. ½ cup) warm water and set aside. Sift dry ingredients into a warm bowl. Add eggs, yeast mixture and remaining water and mix.

Knead on a floured board until smooth and spongy. In a warm place set aside, covered with a towel, to rise for about 1 hour. Knead again and return to rise until doubled in bulk. Divide dough in two and cut each half into three parts. Roll into ropes. Fasten three ropes at one end and braid together fastening when finished. Place on greased baking sheets or in loaf pans, cover again and set aside once more to double in bulk.

Brush with glaze, sprinkle with seeds and bake in a moderate oven (375°F. or Gas Mark 5) until golden.

Braided for Sabbath, in round pyramid shape for Rosh Hashono, and five times normal size for Purim when it is called Keylitch.

Butter buns

BILKES, BARCHES, BOBKES
BUTTER BUNS

Cooking time   30 minutes
To make   30 buns

You will need

1 oz. fresh yeast
⅘ pint (U.S. 2 cups) warm milk
12 oz. sugar
½ teaspoon salt
2 lb. flour, sifted
8 oz. butter
3 eggs, beaten
raisins and nuts
melted butter

TO GLAZE

1 egg yolk
2 tablespoons water

Dissolve yeast in warm milk and add 4 oz. sugar, salt and 4 oz. flour. Beat well and set aside in a warm place to rise while you proceed. Cream the butter and remaining sugar. Beat in the eggs, one at a time, and add to first mixture. Mix raisins and nuts into remaining flour and add, mixing well. Cover and let rise until doubled in bulk. Shape into balls and fit them next to one another in a large baking pan, putting a bit of melted butter between each bun. Put to rise again for 2 hours. Brush with diluted egg yolk and bake in a moderately hot oven (400°F. or Gas Mark 6) for about 30 minutes. Serve warm.

PITA
PANCAKE BREAD

(Illustrated in colour on page 57)
Cooking time   10 —15 minutes
To make   20 pitas

You will need

1 oz. fresh yeast
1 teaspoon sugar
½ pint (U.S. 1¼ cups) lukewarm water
1 lb. flour
1 teaspoon salt

Dissolve the yeast and sugar in the water. Sift flour and salt and add dissolved yeast mixture. Knead and then divide into 20 balls. Roll each out thinly on a floured board. Cover and set to rise for 30 minutes. Roll out thinly once more and set to rise for another 30 minutes. Bake in a very hot oven (500°F. or Gas Mark 9) for only a few minutes, until puffed up and slightly browned. When cut in halves the pita, being hollow, is like an envelope. This bread is from the Middle East.

KAYEK
SALT SESAME BISCUITS (U.S. COOKIES)

Cooking time   20 minutes
To make   20 biscuits (U.S. cookies)

You will need

14 oz. flour
2 teaspoons baking powder
scant ¼ pint (U.S. ½ cup) water
2 eggs
3 tablespoons oil
1 tablespoon salt
2½ oz. sesame seeds

Mix all the ingredients together. Thinly roll dough and cut into cracker-sized squares. Bake in a moderately hot oven (375°F. or Gas Mark 5) until biscuits (U.S. cookies) are light gold in colour and crisp in texture — about 20 minutes.
A Syrian break-the-fast Yum Kippur 'bread' that is crisp.

ZEMEL-PAMPALIK

FLAT ONION BREAD

(Illustrated in colour on opposite page)

Cooking time   20 minutes
To make   6 zemels

You will need

$\frac{2}{5}$ pint (U.S. 1 cup) warm water
1 teaspoon salt
1 tablespoon sugar
1 tablespoon oil
$\frac{1}{2}$ oz. dried yeast in 1 tablespoon warm water
12 oz. flour
1 egg beaten lightly
coarse salt and chopped onion for sprinkling

To the warm water add salt, sugar and oil, then wait until lukewarm before adding the dissolved yeast. Add flour gradually, sifting and mixing. Knead until smooth and springy. Cover and leave overnight in a warm place.
In the morning knead the dough and cut into balls (about tennis ball size) and roll out to about $\frac{1}{2}$-inches thickness.
Brush with egg yolk diluted in 2 tablespoons water and sprinkle with coarse salt and chopped onion. Pierce the dough with a fork.
Bake on a floured pan in a moderately hot oven (400°F. or Gas Mark 6) for about 20 minutes until onions are brown and crusts crisp and golden.

BAGELS

CRUSTY RINGS

(Illustrated in colour on opposite page)

Cooking time   30 minutes
To make   30 bagels

You will need

4 tablespoons oil
2 tablespoons sugar
$\frac{1}{2}$ teaspoon salt
$\frac{2}{5}$ pint (U.S. 1 cup) warm water
$\frac{1}{2}$ oz. dried yeast
1 egg
15 oz. flour, sifted

Mix the oil, sugar and salt with the warm water and after it cools to lukewarm add the yeast and stir. Beat the egg until frothy, add it to the liquid and then mix in the flour. Knead the dough and shape into doughnuts. Cover and set aside to rise on a floured board. When bagels begin to swell, drop them, one at a time, into briskly boiling water and cook until they rise to the top and are light. Place these on oiled baking tins and bake in a moderately hot oven (400°F. or Gas Mark 6) until crisp and golden — about 25 minutes.

Note

For Sunday breakfasts in the U.S.A. this crusty ring is split, spread with cream cheese and smoked salmon.

Sabbath and festival bread   1
Sweet braided Sabbath bread 2
Daily sesame bun   3
Braided Sabbath bun   4

5   Daily poppyseed bun
6   Flat onion bread
7   A pile of pancake bread
8   Crusty rings

A selection of breads

Sephardic baked fish

FISH

DAGIM

Get six Jewish women together to talk about recipes for gefilte fish and you will have six arguments running high on how much pepper and onion to use and whether or not to add a hint or a dose or no sugar! Traditional as this dish is among Central and East European Jewry, who took it to all lands over the New World of the West, Jewish housewives from the Far and Near East had never heard of it. Instead, they have a Sephardic fish to offer which differed little from one Oriental land to another. Reason: their source was the same.

When Jews fled from the persecution and inquisition of Spain in the fifteenth century, they took their culinary art with them to many parts of Western Asia. Now that the remnant of Central Europe's Jews have come to Israel, and most of the Jews from Arab lands have fled to the Holy Land, there is quite a meeting of the Ashkenazic and Sephardic menus, but no hodge-podge dish has, fortunately, resulted from the altering of these two traditional recipes.

Carp ponds abound in Israel today. Fishermen still cast nets on the Sea of Galilee, which is really a lake, as they have done for thousands of years, and fishing boats go far out to sea. Jewish cooking of fish dishes from communities all over the world can now be had in Israel. The Rumanian fish giuvetch, the Alsatian sweet-sour fish and the Dutch fish cakes, are becoming as popular everywhere as the Jewish scharfe fish. But the native Israelis have their own specialities such as St. Peter's fish from Lake Gennosaret grilled on embers as in Bible times, and fish Saniya which is dressed in their much-loved Tahina.

KARPION B'PAPRIKA

CARP IN PAPRIKA

Cooking time 1 hour
To serve 8

You will need

4 sweet fleshy green peppers
1 lb. fresh tomatoes
4 lb. fresh carp
1½ teaspoons salt
5⅓ oz. finely chopped onions
4 oz. margarine
1½ teaspoons paprika
4 tablespoons water

Chop the sweet green peppers and chop the tomatoes.

Cut the carp into serving pieces. Sprinkle the fish with the salt.

Lightly fry the finely chopped onions in the margarine, stirring often. Sprinkle with the paprika and add the water. Cook until the onions become mushy. Add the chopped green peppers and the chopped tomatoes and bring to the boil.

Place the fish in a baking dish and pour on the paprika sauce. Bake for about 45 minutes in a moderate oven (350°F. or Gas Mark 4), basting from time to time.

Carp in paprika is of Hungarian-Austrian origin.

SCHARFE FISH

SAVOURY FISH IN EGG SAUCE

Cooking time   45 minutes
To serve   8

You will need

4 lb. any variety fish
water
1 teaspoon sugar
salt and pepper
1 celery root or 4 stalks
3 onions
3 carrots
3 egg yolks
1½ oz. butter or margarine
dash mace
chopped parsley

Cut the fish into serving pieces and cover with water. Add sugar, salt and pepper and the vegetables. Cook until fish is done (about 30 minutes) and remove the fish to a serving dish. Continue cooking vegetables until liquid is diminished to about ⁴⁄₅ pint (U.S. 2 cups). Remove vegetables and strain the liquid. Pour a little of the liquid into the beaten egg yolks and then return this to the saucepan with all the liquid. Cook over very low heat or in a double boiler, stirring constantly until thick. Do not boil. Add butter or margarine and cook until thick. Season with mace and chopped parsley and pour over the fish. Serve cold.
A cold dish for the Sabbath third meal, 'Seudah Shlishit'.

MOOSHT B'GHALIM

BARBECUED ST. PETER'S FISH

Cooking time   20 minutes
To serve   6

You will need

12 8-inch St. Peter's fish (or trout)
oil as needed
4 onions, cut into thick slices
parsley sprigs
salt and pepper
dash cayenne (optional)
lemon juice as needed

Barbecued St Peter's fish

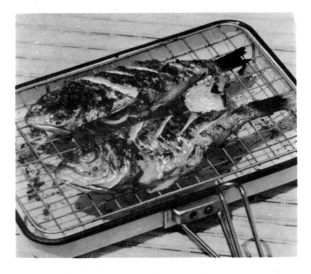

Oil the rack over your barbecue grill. Brush the fishes, inside and out, with oil, and sprinkle with salt, cayenne and pepper and put a slice of onion and a sprig of parsley in the cavity of each fish. Grill over the embers, browning well before turning. Sprinkle on lemon juice and oil during grilling. Cook for about 15 minutes until fish are done. A fish still served at the Sea of Galilee, as in biblical days.

KARPION MEVUSHAL
BOILED CARP

Cooking time   30 minutes
To serve   6

You will need

3 lb. fresh carp
1½ tablespoons coarse salt
3 large onions, sliced
3 carrots, sliced
1 lb. celery root, sliced
2 parsnip roots, sliced
2 tomatoes, halved
pepper to taste
1¼ tablespoons sugar
fine salt, to taste
water

Sprinkle the freshly killed carp with coarse salt and put aside for 30 minutes then rinse well. Put the sliced vegetables in a fish kettle and then put the fish, whole or cut into portions, on top. On the

Boiled carp

fish put the halved tomatoes and seasoning. Cover with water and cook until the fish is done — about 30 minutes. Remove fish to a serving dish. Strain the stock over it. The fish may be served hot or cold (it then jellifies), with the vegetables on the side.

Karpion mevushal is the most popular fish dish in Israel made of pond carp, cooked within hours after killing.

GIPIKILTE FISH
PICKLED FISH

Cooking time   35 minutes
To serve   12

You will need

⅖ pint (U.S. 1 cup) white wine vinegar
⅖ pint (U.S. 1 cup) water
1 tablespoon salt
4 bay leaves
12 peppercorns
3 cloves
8 allspice seeds
1 teaspoon celery seed
½ teaspoon mustard seed
4 onions, sliced
6 lb. fish, cut into 12 pieces

Boil together the vinegar, water, seasoning, spices and onions. Put the fish into this liquid and cook over a low heat for about 30 minutes. Let the fish cool in the stock and then remove it to a glass jar. Strain the stock and pour over the fish. Serve cold.

This dish of Baltic source is often served as post-fast food after Yom Kippur.

Note
This fish keeps for about a month in the refrigerator, its flavour improving from day to day.

DAG MITZRI KAHROOSH
JELLIED LEMON FISH

Cooking time   35 minutes
To serve   6

You will need

6 tablespoons olive oil
3 cloves garlic, chopped
generous 1 pint (U.S. 3 cups) water
juice 3 lemons
salt and pepper
2 teaspoons curry powder (optional)
1 tablespoon sugar
5 tablespoons chopped parsley
6 8-oz. fish steaks

In the hot oil, lightly fry the garlic. Add water, lemon juice, seasonings and parsley. Add the fish steaks and simmer for about 30 minutes until the fish is cooked. Put on to a serving dish and chill. The fish will jellify in its sauce.

An Egyptian dish served cold on the Sabbath.

Jellied lemon fish

GEFILTE FISH (GIFEFIRT)

CHOPPED FISH BALLS, PEPPERY TYPE

Cooking time   1—4 hours
To serve   8

You will need

3 lb. fish (2—3 varieties)
scant 2 pints (U.S. 4½ cups) water
2 teaspoons salt
1 teaspoon white pepper
3 large onions
2 slices white bread or 2 tablespoons
   matzo meal
8 oz. celery root
1 parsnip root
2 large eggs
1 carrot, sliced
onions for layering

Remove the flesh from the fish. Put the bones, head and skin into a fish kettle with scant 1 pint (U.S. 2¼ cups) water, 1 teaspoon salt and ½ teaspoon pepper. Cook briskly. Meanwhile grind the fish with the onion, celery root, parsnip root and bread or matzo meal. Add the eggs, remaining water, salt and pepper. Shape into balls. Put a slice of carrot on each piece of fish. Strain fish bones out of stock. Put a layer of onions into fish kettle and put the fish balls on the onions. Pour the fish stock back into the fish kettle along the side of the vessel so it will not break up the fish balls. Bring to the boil and then reduce heat. If possible simmer fish for 4 hours, though 1 hour will suffice. When cool, strain the stock over the fish, and serve chilled.

This savoury type of gefilte fish is as Russian-Jewish as the sweet type is Polish-Jewish. This recipe is always a source of argument among housewives.

Note

Horseradish beet relish (see page 109) or dill pickles are traditionally served with gefilte fish.

Sweet stuffed fish; chopped fish balls

GEFILTE FISH (ZEESIH)

SWEET STUFFED FISH

(Illustrated in colour on the jacket)
Cooking time   2 hours
To serve   6

You will need

1 3-lb. carp
8 oz. carrots
8 oz. onions
2⅖ pints (U.S. 6 cups) water
2 teaspoons salt
2 hard-boiled eggs
2 raw eggs
1 teaspoon white pepper
3¾ oz. sugar
4 tablespoons oil

Remove the skin in one piece from the fish. This is done by bending back the head of the fish and then separating the flesh from the skin, beginning at the base of the head and working towards the tail. Keep the head attached to the skin. Remove the flesh from the bones. Cook bones with the carrots, onions, water and 1 teaspoon salt for 1 hour; then strain the stock. Put the fish flesh through the mincer together with the hard-boiled eggs. Add the raw eggs, pepper, sugar, oil and remaining salt. Put the filling back into the skin of the fish, and cook it in a fish kettle with the strained stock. Bring to the boil, reduce heat and then cook fish for about 2 hours. Serve cold in slices with the fish jelly.

A Friday night treat of every Western Jewish home.

Note
Any freshwater fleshy fish can be used instead of carp. Two varieties of fish are often mixed together for the stuffing.

Sweet-sour fish

DAG KAROOSH B'SHAMENET
JELLIED COD IN SOUR CREAM

No cooking
To serve   8

You will need

2 tablespoons powdered gelatine
scant ¼ pint (U.S. ½ cup) hot fish stock
2 lb. flaked cooked cod or other fish
generous ½ pint (U.S. 1¼ cups) sour cream,
  mixed with mayonnaise to taste
1 teaspoon grated horseradish
salt and pepper to taste
chopped onion (optional)

Dissolve the gelatine in the hot fish stock and mix with remaining ingredients. Chill in a fish mould or in deep patty tin. Unmould and serve on lettuce with a garnishing of vegetables.

Suitable for Shavuot or for summer meals.

ZEESIH-ZOYIRIH FISH
SWEET-SOUR FISH

Cooking time   40 minutes
To serve   7—9

You will need

10½ oz. chopped onions
1 3-lb. freshwater fish
2 teaspoons salt
water
2 oz. gingerbread crumbs
scant ¼ pint (U.S. ½ cup) white wine
4 oz. sugar
5 tablespoons raisins
juice 1½ lemons
1 lemon, sliced

Put the onions in a fish kettle and lay the fish on it. Sprinkle with salt and cover with water. If you like, make incisions for portions. Simmer until fish is done — about 30 minutes — and then put into a serving dish. Strain off generous ½ pint (U.S. 1¼ cups) of the stock and add remaining ingredients except lemon slices to this liquid. Cook until thick and smooth. Pour sauce over the fish and serve hot or cold and garnish with raisins and lemon slices.

An old traditional Sabbath dish from Alsace and Switzerland.
Note
For a more pungent flavour lemon slices may be boiled in the sauce.

Jellied cod in sour cream

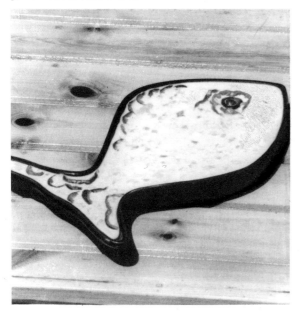

DAG-LIMON TUNISI
LEMONED FISH

Cooking time 30 minutes
To serve 6

You will need

3 lb. any kind small fish
⅛ pint (U.S. ⅓ cup) oil
1 teaspoon salt
dash cayenne pepper
dash saffron
water
juice 1½ lemons
12 new small potatoes or sliced cooked
  potatoes
12 small young onions
1 sliced lemon

Put the fish into an ovenproof dish. Sprinkle the fish with the oil, salt and the cayenne pepper. Dissolve the saffron in 1 tablespoon of hot water for 5 minutes. Add the lemon juice. Sprinkle this mixture on to the fish. Surround with the potatoes and onions. Cover the fish with lemon slices. Add water to almost cover the contents. Bake in a moderately hot oven (400°F. or Gas Mark 6) for about 30 minutes, until vegetables are done. Baste the fish during baking.

This is a Tunisian dish in Jewish cuisine.

Lemoned fish

DAG-VARDIT METUGAN
PETITE PANDORA FISH
DEEP FRIED

Cooking time 10 minutes
To serve 6

You will need

12 Pandoras or other small fish such as
  sardines, bleak, herrings, etc.
prepared mustard for spreading
juice 1 lemon
dash salt and pepper
flour
2 eggs
dry breadcrumbs
deep oil for frying
lemon wedges

Wipe the fish and then spread with prepared mustard diluted with lemon juice. Sprinkle with salt and pepper and roll in the flour. Beat eggs and then dip the fish in the egg. Roll in breadcrumbs. Fry in hot deep fat until golden and crisp on the outside. Drain and serve with lemon wedges.
There are many spicing nuances in deep frying fish; this one is with the Yugoslavian-Jewish flavour.

DAG-FILAI MITOOGAHN
PAN FRIED FISH FILLETS

Cooking time 8 minutes
To serve 6

You will need

salt and pepper
celery salt or paprika or mace
1 egg
3 tablespoons milk or water
2 lb. fish fillets (cod, hake or halibut)
cornmeal or breadcrumbs
oil for frying

Mix the seasoning with the lightly beaten egg diluted in the milk or water. Dip the fish fillets in the egg mixture, then roll in cornmeal or breadcrumbs. Fry in the hot fat until brown — about 8 minutes. Garnish to taste.
This is an everyday dish of every Israeli family.

Pan fried fish fillets

Baked fish with sesame paste

DAG SINAYA
BAKED FISH
WITH SESAME PASTE

Cooking time   20 minutes
To serve   6

You will need

1 5-lb. fish or
  6 8-oz. fishes *
salt and pepper
oil
3 large onions
8 oz. tahina paste (see page 18)
3 tablespoons chopped parsley

* Any kind of fresh or salt water fish can be used
  in this dish.

Make 2 slashes in the skin of each small fish or
several slashes if a larger fish and sprinkle with salt
and pepper. Fry the fish lightly in oil and then put
into a baking dish. Fry the onions in the same oil
and put them on the fish. Spoon the prepared
tahina paste over the fish then sprinkle over the
chopped parsley.
Bake for 20 minutes in a moderately hot oven
(375°F. or Gas Mark 5) until the tahina is golden.
Serve hot.

This is a favourite dish in Mediterranean Jewish
households.

GIBROOTINI GEFILTE FISH
OVEN-FRIED GEFILTE FISH

Cooking time   45 minutes
To serve   6

You will need

4 eggs
2 slices white bread
1 lb. carp fillets
1 lb. fish fillets of any other kind
1 celery root
1 carrot
2 onions
2 teaspoons salt
$\frac{1}{3}$ teaspoon pepper
oil for baking

Boil 2 of the eggs until hard. Soak the slices of
white bread in water and squeeze dry.
Put the hard-boiled eggs, the bread, the carp
fillets and other fish, the celery root, the carrot
and the onions through the mincer.
Add the rest of the ingredients and mix them well.
Form the mixture into patties. Heat the oil in
a roasting pan and put in the patties.
Bake for about 45 minutes in a moderately hot
oven (400°F. or Gas Mark 6) until fish is browned,
turning once.
Serve hot or cold.

DAG GIUVETCH
FISH AND VEGETABLE STEW

(Illustrated on opposite page)

Cooking time about 1 hour
To serve 10

You will need

2 lb. root vegetables (carrots, turnips,
  celery root, parsnip, etc.)
1 lb. potatoes
1 lb. tomatoes
4 oz. onions
1 clove garlic
1 lb. other vegetables (peas, string beans,
  green peppers, cabbage)
salt and pepper to taste
⅖ pint (U.S. 1 cup) water
4 lb. any kind fish
4 tablespoons oil
4 tablespoons flour

Dice the root vegetables, the potatoes, the tomatoes
and the onions. Chop the other vegetables.
Put all the vegetables, salt and pepper and water
into a saucepan and cook until potatoes are almost
tender.
Cut fish up into serving pieces, brush with oil
and roll in flour. Put the fish on the vegetables.
Continue to cook for another 30 minutes, basting
the fish with the sauce.
If you like, the fish can be put in whole at the beginning and vegetables can be arranged and cooked
in an ornamental pattern.
A Rumanian dish.

DAG AFOOYIH, SEPHARDI
SEPHARDIC BAKED FISH

(Illustrated in colour on page 58)

Cooking time about 50 minutes
To serve 8

You will need

1 5-lb. sea fish or 2 smaller fish
salt and pepper
6 onions, chopped
2 cloves garlic, chopped
1 small chilli pepper, cut up
7 tablespoons olive oil
5 tablespoons chopped parsley
8 tomatoes chopped
lemon juice
dash curry powder or turmeric
water
8 tablespoons pine nuts

Place the fish, uncut, into a buttered baking dish
and sprinkle with the salt and pepper. Fry the
onions, garlic and chilli pepper in 6 tablespoons oil.
Sprinkle these over the fish and then sprinkle on
the parsley. Lightly fry the tomatoes and put over
the fish. Mix lemon juice and curry powder or
turmeric and add enough water to almost cover
the fish. Bake the fish for about 45 minutes or till
tender in a moderate oven (350°F. or Gas Mark 4).
Baste fish from time to time during baking. Lightly
fry the pine nuts in 1 tablespoon oil and sprinkle
over the fish.
Jews of the Sephardic Community all relish this
baked fish.

Fish and vegetable stew

POULTRY

OAFOT

A Jewish witticism says that chicken is never served on a weekday unless someone is ill or the chicken is sick! And indeed that was the case among the poor Jewish masses of Eastern Europe for generations.

It was also so in Israel during the days of austerity just after the State was reborn. With acute rationing the settled population tightened its belt so that we could absorb our survivors from Europe after Hitler's massacres, and Jewish refugees from Arab lands. Within a few years our population trebled with such immigrants, all destitute on arrival. Our chicken allotment came to about one per person per year, and so a joke made the rounds that we should use it only as a cock crow to wake us for work early in the morning, as was done in Bible times!

Today Israel's poultry production is so great that we export to much of Europe and at home it is an everyday dish. This abundance and the quality of local poultry has resulted in the creating and adaptation of many fascinating dishes. The olde-tyme 'chicken in the pot' which was about the only way our parents served the dish, is still enjoyed (but not often served, as being plain and unexciting).

Our Jaffa orange crop and other fruits have brought such dishes as 'chicken in orange' and 'pomegranate or grape-juiced chicken' into popularity. The much loved sesame seed usually reserved for cakes and confections has also been applied to make a wonderful sesame chicken.

Many savoury and piquant nuances have also been introduced to poultry dishes in Jewish cuisine. The abundant use of celery, the flavouring with chopped vegetables and spice ranging from cinnamon to garlic and curry have done wonders to tone up old Jewish recipes.

KATCHKEH

ROAST DUCK

Cooking time   1½ hours
To serve   4

You will need

1 4-lb. duck
2 cloves garlic, crushed
salt and pepper
2 apples, halves
celery stalks and leaves
scant ¼ pint (U.S. ½ cup) water

Rub the duck, inside and out, with the crushed garlic and sprinkle with salt and pepper. Put the halved apples and celery stalks and leaves in the cavity of the bird. These are for flavouring only and are removed before serving. Put the duck on a rack in a baking pan into a preheated very hot oven (450°F. or Gas Mark 8) and cover for first 30 minutes. Reduce the heat to 325°F. or Gas Mark 2—3. Drain off the fat and put in the water. Continue cooking without a cover for about 1 hour, basting from time to time so the bird will brown nicely and not dry out.

Germanic Jewry added their own nuance to roast duck.

Roast duck

pomegranate or grape juice from time to time to flavour, colour and glaze the bird. Serve garnished with mounds of grapes or pomegranate seeds.

This Georgian dish is a Sabbath favourite.

OAF GROOZEE MIMULAH
GEORGIAN STUFFED CHICKEN

(Illustrated in colour on the jacket)
Cooking time   about 3½ hours
To serve   6

You will need

3 medium-sized onions, chopped
3 tablespoons oil
scant ¼ pint (U.S. ½ cup) water
8 oz. chopped beef
¼ teaspoon freshly ground pepper
½ teaspoon cinnamon
¼ teaspoon allspice
1 teaspoon salt
⅖ pint (U.S. 1 cup) pomegranate or
   grape juice
1 tablespoon sugar
3 tablespoons lemon juice
1 3-lb. roasting chicken
½ lemon
grapes or pomegranate seeds

Fry the onions until golden in the oil. Add the water to the beef, stir in the onions and cook until the water has evaporated, stirring from time to time. Drain off any fat left in the pan. Add the spices and salt to the meat mixture. Pour in the pomegranate or grape juice and add the sugar and lemon juice. Rub the chicken, inside and out, with the lemon and then fill with the meat stuffing. Lightly brown the chicken in the remaining oil. Pot roast it on very low heat for about 3 hours, adding more

GIKOCHTEH HINDEL
CHICKEN IN THE POT

Cooking time   about 2 hours
To serve   6—8

You will need

½ oz. chicken fat
3 onions, thinly sliced
1 stewing chicken, cut up *
salt, pepper, paprika

* Chicken can be cooked whole in this manner.

Put the chicken fat and onions in a saucepan with the chicken pieces on top. Sprinkle with seasoning. Firmly put a lid on the saucepan and cook over a very low fire. Water should not be added unless the chicken is fat, and even then only a few spoonfuls should be added at a time, for this traditional dish is best stewed in its own juice. Cook until the chicken is tender — about 2 hours, depending on age of bird. Serve with carrot tzimmis and knaidlach (see pages 30 and 32) as is the custom.

Chicken in the pot

TARNEGOL HODU IM FARFEL

ROAST TURKEY WITH FARFEL FILLING

Cooking time 5 hours
To serve 15

You will need

1 10-lb. turkey
salt and white pepper
margarine as needed
water for roasting

SWEET FARFEL FILLING

1 lb. 2 oz. raw farfel
4 oz. margarine
scant ¼ pint (U.S. 1 cup) fruit juice
   (orange preferably)
5¼ oz. raisins or 12 prunes (soaked)
2 apples, chopped
grated rind 1 lemon
6 tablespoons sugar
dash cinnamon
dash nutmeg

SAVOURY FARFEL FILLING

3 cups raw farfel
2 oz. chicken fat or oil
scant ¼ pint (U.S. 1 cup) chicken soup
6 tablespoons chopped onion
1 egg, beaten
1 teaspoon salt
dash pepper, paprika, nutmeg
4 tablespoons chopped parsley
1 lb. diced celery stalk or root
1 carrot, coarsely grated
sweet stuffings for Rosh Hashono — savoury
stuffings for other festivals.

Rub the turkey with salt and soft margarine inside
and out, and sprinkle with a little white pepper.
For the stuffing (whether sweet or savoury) fry the
farfel in the fat, then add the liquid and cook until
absorbed. Add the remaining ingredients and put
into the cavity of the bird. Sew up or fasten with
skewers. Roast the turkey with a little water in the
pan in a slow oven (300°F. or Gas Mark 2) until
browned and tender, basting from time to time.
About 30 minutes is required for each 1 lb. turkey.

OAF KARPAS

CHICKEN CELERIAC

Cooking time 1—1½ hours
To serve 6

You will need

1 3-lb. young chicken
scant ¼ pint (U.S. ½ cup) oil
10 small onions
1 lb. celery or celeriac root, cubed *
scant ¼ pint (U.S. ½ cup) tomato purée
salt and pepper to taste
scant ½ pint (U.S. 1 cup) water
2 bundles celery, stalks and leaves

* If you use a generous sprinkling of celery salt
.you can use less celery.

Lightly fry the whole chicken in oil and put it into
a heavy saucepan with the onions, celery root,
tomato purée, seasoning and water. Cover with wet
leaves and stalks of celery and put a lid firmly on
the saucepan. Cook over very low heat for about
1—1½ hours until vegetables and chicken are
tender. Wet the celery from time to time with a
sprinkling of water.
Of North African origin, this has been widely
introduced to Israel.

HABOUSHIM MEMULAIM

QUINCES STUFFED WITH CHICKEN

Cooking time 1½ hours
To serve 6

You will need

12 small quinces
4 chicken breasts
3 tablespoons matzo meal or breadcrumbs
dash cinnamon or cloves
dash salt
margarine
sugar

Peel and core the quinces. Leave the bottom of the
fruit intact but make the cavity as large as possible.
Grind the chicken meat, mix with the breadcrumbs or matzo meal and add the spice and salt.
Fill the quinces with this mixture and top with a pat

Quinces stuffed with chicken

of margarine. Put into a baking dish with a little water on the bottom. Sprinkle with sugar and bake in a hot oven (400°F. or Gas Mark 6) for about 1½ hours ot until quinces are pink and cooked.

A Persian dish that comes to table on Sabbath eve when quinces are in season.

OAF-TAPUZIM

ORANGED CHICKEN

Cooking time 50 minutes
To serve 6

You will need

generous ¾ pint (U.S. 2 cups) orange juice
2 tablespoons grated orange rind
4 oz. brown sugar
1½ oz. margarine, melted
1 tablespoon prepared mustard
1 4-lb. young chicken split down the back
1½ tablespoons cornflour
2 tablespoons cold water

TO GARNISH

orange slices

Mix orange juice, rind, and brown sugar. Mix melted margarine with the mustard and rub over chicken. Open up the chicken and put it (skin side down) in a greased baking pan and pour over the orange juice mixture.

Bake in a hot oven (425°F. or Gas Mark 7) for about 45 minutes until chicken is tender. Baste the bird frequently. For the last 15 minutes of the baking have the skin side up to brown and glaze.
Dissolve cornflour in cold water, add to gravy and cook until thick.
Serve with a garnish of orange slices.
An Israeli dish, born of its large production of oranges and poultry.

Note

For a touch of fun, chicken can be made to look like a girl in a bikini, dancing the twist.

HAMIM IRAQI

SABBATH IRAQI CHOLENT

Cooking time 12 hours
To serve 6

You will need

9 oz. broad or navy beans or chick peas
1 fat boiling fowl
3½ oz. rice
3 tablespoons oil
10 large tomatoes, cut up
sprinkling cinnamon
sprinkling cardamom or cumin
salt and pepper
water to cover
6 oz. burghul (see page 44) or more rice
1 lb. winter hard squash, pumpkin or carrots

Soak the beans or chick peas for 6 hours. Skin the chicken from below the wings, to include the wings and skin of the neck. Fry the rice in the oil until golden, add 4 of the diced tomatoes with a sprinkling of cinnamon (cardamom or cumin), salt and pepper. Fill the cavity of the skin with rice about one-third full and sew up. Put the drained beans or chick peas in a saucepan with the skinned chicken, and the stuffed skin next to it. Surround with burghul and vegetables. Sprinkle with more spice, salt and pepper. Top with the remaining tomatoes. Cover with water and simmer on very low heat overnight.
Serve after Synagogue service on the Sabbath.

This dish stews overnight to avoid preparation on the Sabbath.

OAF L'MELECH

KOSHER CHICKEN À LA KING

Cooking time 1 hour
To serve 6

You will need

1 3½-lb. chicken
water
3½ oz. margarine
3 tablespoons flour
generous ½ pint (U.S. 1½ cups) chicken stock *
scant ¼ pint (U.S. ½ cup) white wine
dash white pepper
1 teaspoon salt
dash nutmeg
1 sweet green pepper
1 sweet red pepper
2½ oz. sliced mushrooms
2 egg yolks

* If there is no chicken stock available it is possible to use 1 chicken bouillon cube and enough water to make up to the desired amount of required liquid.

Cut up the chicken and cook with enough water to cover until the meat is tender and can be removed from the bone.
Cut chicken meat into 1-inch cubes.
Boil the stock down to a generous ½ pint (U. S. 1½ cups).
Melt 1½ oz. margarine, add the flour, and when it begins to bubble gradually add the stock and wine and stir until thickened and smooth.
Add the pepper, salt and nutmeg.
Cut the red and green peppers into fine slivers and fry lightly in 1½ oz. margarine, then add the mushrooms and fry for 5 minutes. If cooked mushrooms are used, then fry only for 1 minute.
Add the vegetables to the chicken and keep hot.
Put the sauce into a blender. Slowly add the remaining margarine and egg yolks and blend until white. Add the sauce to the remaining ingredients and mix carefully.
Serve in pastry shells or on rice.

Note

This American dish, made in the original with cream and fowl, has been altered to conform to Jewish Kashrut laws and has become very popular.

Celeried turkey patties

TARNEGOL HODU B'KARPAS
CELERIED TURKEY PATTIES

Cooking time about 1 hour
To serve 6

You will need

2 lb. celery root (celeriac)
3 oz. chicken fat
2 celery stalks
2 lb. turkey breasts
3 eggs
1 teaspoon salt
dash nutmeg or cinnamon
3 slices white bread
water as needed

Thinly slice the celery root and fry lightly in the fat.
Grind the celery stalks and turkey breasts and add the eggs, salt and nutmeg or cinnamon.
Soak the bread, squeeze dry and add to the above mixture.
Shape the mixture into flat round patties and fry only for a couple of minutes until slightly golden, then place each patty on a round of celery root.
Add only enough water to cover the bottom of the pot; add more during cooking as needed and simmer for about 1 hour, turning the patties two or three times during the cooking.

The ingredients are basically American, but the dish is Tunisian.

KEFTELE ROMANI
RUMANIAN CHICKEN CAKES

Cooking time   30 minutes
To serve   6 — 7

You will need

1 lb. chicken breasts
4 onions
salt to taste
oil for frying
12 green pears, cut up
water to cover
6 eggs, beaten

Put the chicken breasts and onions through a mincer, add salt and fry in the oil. Peel and cut up the pears. Cover with water and cook for 10 minutes. Drain. Add the pears to the chicken mixture with the eggs. Fry like pancakes.
This delicate Rumanian dish is served on Passover with the traditional fiery beetroot-horseradish relish.

JEDJAD ZEITOON
OLIVE CHICKEN

Cooking time   30 minutes
To serve   6

You will need

1 young 3-lb. chicken
4 tablespoons olive oil
sprinkling saffron or turmeric
water
6 oz. green olives, pitted (or more)
1 sweet pickled lemon (see page 110) *
1 clove garlic

* You can substitute a peeled fresh lemon, and add 3 tablespoons of sugar, though taste is somewhat different from the pickled lemon.

Cut the chicken into serving pieces. Brush with the oil and sprinkle with saffron or turmeric diluted in 1 tablespoon water. Put chicken into a heavy saucepan and cover with the olives and slices of pickled lemon and the crushed garlic. Cover with water and simmer for about 30 minutes until the chicken is tender.
A much loved dish of Moroccan Jewry.

POLPETTONE DI TACCHINO
STUFFED TURKEY BREAST

Cooking time   1½ hours
To serve   6

You will need

1 whole turkey breast, without wings
4 tablespoons soft breadcrumbs
2 eggs
salt and pepper
dash oregano or sweet basil
chicken soup to cover

TO GARNISH

6 hard-boiled eggs
parsley

Have your butcher remove most of the turkey flesh. Mince the meat, mix with the breadcrumbs, eggs, salt, pepper and oregano. Fill the skin and sew it up. Puncture with a needle so the skin will not burst during cooking. Stew in the chicken soup for 1½ hours. Serve cold with a garnish of halved hard-boiled eggs and parsley.
An Italian cold-cut served after the Yom Kippur fast.

OAF MIZRACHI
ORIENTAL CHICKEN

Cooking time   45 minutes — 1 hour
To serve   6

You will need

1 3-lb. chicken
scant ¼ pint (U.S. ½ cup) olive or other oil
1 clove garlic, minced
2 onions, chopped
12 oz. chopped tomatoes
1 green pepper, chopped
1 tablespoon pine nuts
scant ½ pint (U.S. 1 cup) water
dash turmeric or curry (optional)
1 chilli pepper (optional)

Cut the chicken into serving pieces and brown in the oil. Put into a casserole with the oil. Add remaining ingredients and bake in a hot oven (375°F. or Gas Mark 5) for about 30—45 minutes or until chicken is tender.

OAF SUM-SUM

SESAME CHICKEN

(Illustrated in colour on page 76)
Cooking time   40 minutes
To serve   6

You will need

4 oz. flour
5¼ oz. sesame seeds
2 teaspoons paprika
2 teaspoons salt
1 2½-lb. frying chicken
1 egg
scant ½ pint (U.S. 1 cup) stock or water
oil for frying

Mix the flour, sesame seeds, paprika and salt in
a paper bag.
Cut the chicken into serving pieces and shake in the
bag. Beat the egg and add to the stock. Dip the
chicken in this liquid and then shake again in the
bag. Heat the oil in a pan and fry the chicken until
just golden.
Put chicken into a baking dish and bake in a warm
oven (350°F. or Gas Mark 4) for about 30 minutes
or until tender.
Serve on boiled rice garnished with black olives.

Sesame seeds are a Middle Eastern favourite in
many foods.

DUAZ FEHNJOH

GLAZED GOOSE

Cooking time   2—3 hours
To serve   8

You will need

1 8-lb. goose
scant ¼ pint (U.S. ½ cup) lemon juice
4 tablespoons honey
dash allspice or cinnamon
dash salt
8 very small apples
16 blanched almonds
8 teaspoons sugar
4 tablespoons icing sugar
mint sprigs

Brush the goose inside and out with the lemon juice
and set aside for 30 minutes. Rub the goose, inside
and out, with the honey and sprinkle with allspice
or cinnamon, and salt. Core, but do not peel, the
apples and fill the holes with blanched almonds and
sugar. Stuff into the cavity of the goose. Fasten with
skewers. Roast the goose on the spit for about 2—2½
hours, or in a moderate oven (350°F. or Gas
Mark 4) about 2¾—3 hours. When done, sprinkle
with icing sugar and return to the oven for 5 minutes. Serve garnished with sprigs of mint.

A festive Persian dish for Rosh Hashono.

74

Grilled meat on skewers

Sesame chicken

MEAT

BAHSAHR

Chapter 11 of Leviticus relates what animal foods are permitted; those forbidden are classified as unclean and an abomination. Many of these ordained rules have been backed in modern times by science as healthy. Among warm-blooded animals, birds of prey are forbidden and abhorred.

The only beasts permitted for food are quadrupeds with cloven hoofs who also chew the cud, thus limiting even grass-eating animals to cattle, deer, sheep and goats.

Ritual slaughtering as practised under Jewish law is today being applied (except for the prayers) widely in non-kosher commercial meat processing plants. This is done not only because it has been found to be the most painless means of butchering the animal, but because the meat, freed of excessive blood, gains in quality. No diseased animal was ever permitted as food under Jewish laws, and today this caution is applied by governmental supervision in all advanced lands.

The humane approach not to consume blood is another demand of kosher rules. After the ritual slaughtering and inspection, the Jewish housewife completes the koshering process in her own home. The meat is soaked for 30 minutes in cold water, rinsed and then salted and put on a draining board for the blood to run off for an hour. The meat is thereafter rinsed three times.

If grilled, meat need not be koshered as above but a sprinkling of salt must be added to the meat in order to expel the blood. Liver must always be koshered by grilling or broiling with a sprinkling of salt.

Meat may not be mixed with dairy foods because of the humane admonition 'Thou shalt not cook a kid in its mother's milk.'

SHASHLIK

GRILLED MEAT ON SKEWERS

(Illustrated in colour on page 75)

Cooking time   about 10 minutes
To serve   6

You will need

1½ lb. steak
2 cloves garlic
6 tablespoons oil
1 tablespoon lemon juice
salt and pepper

Cut the meat into 1-inch cubes. Mince the garlic and put into the oil with the lemon juice. Marinate the meat in the oil mixture for about 30 minutes, then string the cubes on skewers. Grill over wood coals until edges are browned. Sprinkle with salt and pepper.

Note

Though this can be cooked on any kind of grill, it is the flavour of the wood smoke which makes it taste different.

A dish of Southern Russia and the Near East and most popular of all meat dishes in Israel today.

VARIATION

Liver cubes, kidneys, onions, green peppers, tomatoes or other accompaniments may be put on the skewers along with the steak cubes.

KUFTA-KEFTEDES
EEM TAHINA

HAMBURGERS
WITH SESAME SAUCE

Cooking time   10—15 minutes
To serve   6

You will need

4 tablespoons water
2 teaspoons powdered meat or chicken soup
2 slices bread (without crust)
1½ lb. chopped beef or lamb
2 onions, finely chopped
2 cloves garlic, crushed
salt and pepper to taste
1 teaspoon chopped mint (optional)
1 egg, well beaten
dash cumin, allspice or cinnamon
2 oz. dry breadcrumbs
1 lb. prepared tahina (see page 18)

Mix the water with the soup powder and soak the bread in it. Add the meat, onions, garlic, salt, pepper, mint and egg. Mix well. Add desired spice. Shape into small flat hamburgers and fry or grill until browned. Put these hamburgers into a baking pan or griller. Mix breadcrumbs with prepared tahina sauce and spread on each hamburger. Grill or bake until topping is golden. Serve at once.

Bulgarian Jews spice this with cumin, Moroccans make it fragrant with cinnamon, Syrian Jews use allspice or mint for aroma.

KEBABS

GROUND AND GRILLED LAMB

Cooking time   about 10 minutes
To serve   6—8

You will need

2 lb. lamb, finely minced
2 onions, chopped
1 tablespoon chopped parsley
salt and pepper
pinch cardamom or allspice (optional)
oil

The meat and onions must be finely minced. Add parsley, salt, pepper, and if you wish a pinch of cardamom or allspice. Shape into finger-sized rolls and string on skewers. Sprinkle a little oil over the kebabs and grill them if possible over embers. Serve with minted salad (see page 89) and rice.

A Middle Eastern dish enjoyed all over Israel.

Note
Onion quarters, tomato sections, eggplant cubes, can be strung on the skewers to grill with the kebabs.

GULYAS

VEAL GOULASH STEW

Cooking time   about 1¼ hours
To serve   6

You will need

4 onions, chopped
4 tablespoons oil
3 oz. tomato paste
1 tablespoon paprika
1 teaspoon caraway seeds (optional)
1 teaspoon salt
generous ¾ pint (U.S. 2 cups) water
2 lb. veal, cut in 1-inch cubes
1 tablespoon flour
2 tablespoons water or mild vinegar

Cook the onions in the oil, being careful not to

Veal goulash stew

brown them. Add the tomato paste, paprika, caraway seeds, water and veal. Cook gently until the veal is tender. Dissolve the flour in the water or vinegar and add to the meat. Stir until the sauce has thickened.

Both the Hungarian and the Austrian Veal stews have given birth to the Israel version of this dish.

AHRDY IMPLOODT, PILPEL MIMULA
STUFFED PEPPERS

Cooking time about 1 hour
To serve 6 as a main course
12 as a first course

You will need

12 medium-sized sweet green peppers
1 lb. beef, minced
2½ oz. rice
1 small clove garlic, crushed
1 onion, chopped
salt and pepper
1 tablespoon chicken soup powder (optional)
4 tablespoons wine vinegar
3 tablespoons sugar
generous ¾ pint (U.S. 2 cups) tomato juice
water

Stuffed peppers

Cut off the tops of the peppers and take out the seeds. Mix the beef, rice, garlic, onion, salt and pepper and pack into each pepper to no more than two-thirds and then replace the tops. Fit the peppers together closely into a saucepan. Mix the soup powder, vinegar, sugar and tomato juice and add enough water to just cover the peppers. Bring to the boil and then reduce the heat and cook for about 1 hour until the peppers are tender and about two-thirds of the liquid is absorbed.

VARIATION

You can add a grated carrot to the meat mixture. The flavour of the sauce can also be altered by the addition of garlic or honey.

This dish is of Balkan origin and is served hot or cold as a first or main course.

GEDEMPFTEH FLEISH
STEWED POT ROAST

Cooking time about 2¼ hours
To serve 8

You will need

4 tablespoons oil
3 lb. stewing beef
4 bay leaves
3 onions, sliced
3 cloves garlic, cut up
1 celery or celeriac root, shredded
1 sweet red pepper, diced
1 teaspoon salt
½ teaspoon paprika
⅛ teaspoon cayenne
6 allspice seeds
6 peppercorn seeds
5 oz. tomatoes, chopped
⅖ pint (U.S. 1 cup) water

Heat the oil in a heavy saucepan, then sear the beef in the fat until browned on all sides. Add remaining ingredients. Bring to the boil, then reduce heat to very slow and simmer for about 2 hours until meat is tender. If liquid evaporates add a little water to keep beef from burning. Remove the bay leaves just before serving.

The bay leaf is the crowning touch of this East European dish.

Sabbath beef stew with fruits

CHOLENT MIT FLOHMEN ZIMMES
SABBATH BEEF STEW WITH FRUITS

Cooking time 3½ hours
To serve 6—8

You will need

2 lb. brisket
1 lb. yellow turnips or carrots
1 lb. potatoes
1 lb. prunes
1 tablespoon salt
¼ teaspoon pepper
5 tablespoons honey
juice 1 lemon
water

In a heavy saucepan arrange the meat with the turnips, potatoes and prunes. Mix together the salt, pepper, honey and lemon juice and add. Add sufficient water to cover the meat and vegetables. Cover, bring to the boil and then cook over very low heat for at least 3 hours. Traditionally cholent is left to cook overnight on a very low flame or in a very slow oven (200°F. or Gas Mark 0). Most of the sauce is absorbed and evaporated in the cooking. This cholent is a Central and East European favourite version.

VARIATION
You can substitute sweet potatoes for turnips, dried apricots for prunes and brown sugar for honey. All three or any one or two will produce delightful results.

KATEF SHEL KEVES
ROAST SHOULDER OF LAMB

Cooking time about 2¼ hours
To serve 8

You will need

1 5-lb. shoulder of lamb
2 cloves garlic
3 tablespoons oil
4 sprigs mint (optional)*
salt and pepper
dash chilli powder
scant ¼ pint (U.S. ½ cup) white wine
* Dried mint, steeped in a little hot water and then
  strained, can be used instead of fresh mint.

Rub the lamb with garlic. Brown in hot oil. Put into a roasting pan in a preheated moderately hot oven (400°F. or Gas Mark 6). Sprinkle with salt and pepper and chilli powder and put mint sprigs over the lamb. Add the wine. After 10 minutes reduce heat to 350°F. or Gas Mark 4. Baste from time to time with a little more wine if necessary, or with the pan gravy. Serve with a garnish of fresh mint sprigs.
Traditional on Rosh Hashono in Oriental homes.

VARIATION
Jews of Alsace use the above recipe but add raisins and diced dried pears and apricots, with a whiff of rosemary and 2 tablespoons of sugar, and omit the chilli powder.

Roast shoulder of lamb

Stuffed beef milt

MILTZ

STUFFED BEEF MILT

Cooking time about 1½ hours
To serve 8

You will need

1 beef milt
4 slices white bread
water
6 large onions
1½ oz. margarine
1 teaspoon salt
⅛ teaspoon pepper
dash nutmeg
4 tablespoons oil

With a large knife slit a pocket in the milt until the meat is like a bag. Remove the crusts from the bread, dip in water and squeeze out the liquid. Chop 2 onions and fry in the margarine. Mix the bread, fried onions, salt, pepper and nutmeg and fill the milt with it. Sew up the pocket. Slice the remaining onions and put the stuffed milt on them, sprinkle on the oil, cover with water and stew until the water is almost all absorbed, leaving only enough for a sauce. The milt will come out pot-roasted and brown. Baste and turn 2—3 times during cooking. Serve sliced, hot as a main dish or hors-d'oeuvre.

VARIATION

The milt can also be cooked without stuffing, on a bed of onions, with spicing as above, and stewed and pot-roasted in the same way.

HOLISHKES

MEAT FILLED CABBAGE

Cooking time 50 minutes
To serve 6

You will need

1½ lb. minced beef
6 tablespoons rice
1 egg
2 onions, chopped
salt and pepper
12 cabbage leaves
generous ¼ pint (U.S. ¾ cup) tomato ketchup
  or sauce
water as required

Mix the meat, rice, egg and onions. Season to taste with salt and pepper. Dip the cabbage leaves in hot water to tenderize them. Place a ball of the meat mixture in each leaf and roll up, tucking in the edges. Place in a casserole. Pour on the ketchup or tomato sauce with enough water to cover. Bake in a moderate oven (350°F. or Gas Mark 4) for about 45 minutes until golden on top. If necessary add a little water during baking.

VARIATION

Raisins are often added to the meat mixture. Other names for holishkes are holipces, yaprak, kruv-memulah, praakes and galuptzi.

Meat filled cabbage

Tongue

ZUNGE
TONGUE

Cooking time about 3 hours
To serve 8—10

You will need

1 3-lb. beef tongue
2 cloves
3 allspice
1 bay leaf
2 onions
2 cloves garlic (optional)
3 peppercorns
2 teaspoons salt
water
pinch ginger
2 gingersnaps
3 tablespoons sugar
2 oz. raisins
3 tablespoons wine vinegar
2 tablespoons cornflour
juice 1 lemon (optional)

Cook the tongue (on a low heat, after bringing to
the boil) with the cloves, allspice, bay leaf, onions,
garlic, peppercorns and salt with enough water to
cover for about 2½ hours until tender. Skin the
tongue while still warm and return to the pot with
the strained sauce. Add the ginger, gingersnaps,
sugar, raisins and vinegar and cook for about
20 minutes on a low heat. Mix the cornflour with
3 tablespoons water and add. More sugar may be
added for a sweeter taste, or the juice of a lemon
to add piquancy.

This Alsatian and Swiss dish is a favourite on Rosh
Hashono.

VARIATION
Cook in salt spiced water and remove skin. Serve
cold, thinly sliced.

ROLLADE
ROLLED MARINATED ROAST

Cooking time 2 hours
To serve 8

You will need

3 lb. chuck, rump or flank of beef
scant ¼ pint (U.S. ½ cup) vinegar
2 bay leaves
salt and pepper
dash cloves, ginger
pinch saffron
2 tablespoons drippings
2 large onions, diced
5½ oz. celery root
1 large carrot
scant ¼ pint (U.S. ½ cup) water or wine
2 gingersnaps (optional)

Pound the meat to flatten it a little and then roll
and tie it up. Refrigerate with the vinegar and bay
leaves for a day, turning from time to time. Dry the

Rolled marinated roast

meat and season it. Heat drippings and brown meat on all sides. If necessary, add a little oil to the drippings. Add the vinegar in which the meat has soaked, and the remaining ingredients. Cover. Bring to the boil and then reduce the heat to low and cook for about 2 hours until tender, turning from time to time. The sauce can be thickened by boiling up with crumbed gingersnaps.

A Dutch main dish of the Sabbath, similar to the Austrian Sauerbraten.

Note

This dish is often made of veal, in which case it should only be marinated for half a day and cooked for less time (about 1½ hours).

KLOPS

MEAT-EGG LOAF

Cooking time 1 hour
To serve   6

You will need

2 lb. minced beef
3 slices bread, soaked
2 eggs
4 oz. celery root or parsnip root, grated
scant ¼ pint (U.S. ½ cup) stock or water
1 carrot, grated
2 onions, chopped
2 cloves garlic, crushed
dash nutmeg and allspice
salt and pepper
1 tablespoon parsley, chopped
6 hard-boiled eggs, shelled
margarine

Mix all the ingredients except the hard-boiled eggs and margarine. Put half the mixture into a well-greased loaf pan, then put the whole hard-boiled eggs in a row down the middle of the meat and cover with the remaining meat mixture. Dab top with margarine as desired: a lot if meat is lean, very little if it is fat. Bake for 15 minutes in a very hot oven (500°F. or Gas Mark 9) and then reduce heat to 350°F. or Gas Mark 4 for about 45 minutes until brown and crusted on top. Serve warm or cold in thick slices so the egg centres each piece.
Tomato sauce is very good with this dish.
Served cold at Sabbath brunch by German-Jewish emigrés.

LIENG-LEBER SHTRUDEL

LUNG OR LIVER STRUDEL

Cooking time 40 minutes
To serve   6—8

You will need

3 onions
1½ lb. finely diced cooked beef lung or
    chopped grilled liver, or mixed
3 oz. poultry fat
8 oz. minced boiled meat
salt and pepper
strudel dough, any kind (see pages 128—129)
oil for brushing

Finely dice the onions and cooked beef lung or chopped grilled liver. Fry the onions in the poultry fat until golden. Mix with the remaining ingredients, seasoning to taste — a generous inclusion of pepper is usual.
Spread the filling over the strudel dough. Roll up. Brush with a little oil and bake in a moderately hot oven (400°F. or Gas Mark 6) for about 35 minutes or until golden.

Note

Organ meats were much used by the poor Jews of the Baltic, Balkan and East European lands, but they turned these economy cuts into fine foods.

Lung strudel

SARMI, SARMALI, DOLMA, MALFOUF

STUFFED VINE LEAVES

(Illustrated in colour on opposite page)
Cooking time   about 1 hour
To serve   6

You will need

1 onion, chopped
3 tablespoons olive oil
6 tablespoons raw rice
4 tablespoons pine nuts
12 oz. minced beef
pinch fresh or dried mint
salt and pepper to taste
dash cinnamon
large vine leaves
scant ¼ pint (U.S. ½ cup) white wine
water

Fry the onion in the olive oil, add the rice and fry until golden. Add the pine nuts and toast for a minute. Remove from stove and add the meat, mint, salt, pepper and cinnamon. Dip the grape leaves in hot water to tenderize them. Put a tablespoon of the meat mixture in each leaf and then roll up into finger shapes, tucking in the edges. Put the rolls into a casserole, pour on the wine and add water to cover. Cook over medium heat for about 45 minutes, adding water, if needed, to cover the sarmis. Then allow the liquid to simmer away. Serve hot or cold.
Names for this dish differ with localities, whether Balkan, Asian, Near Eastern or North African, and there are slight alterations in seasoning.

VARIATION

The sarmis can be cooked in a tomato sauce instead of water and wine. Often wine is omitted and more water and seasoning used.

KAHKLEHTEHN

ROAST MEAT BALLS

Cooking time   50 minutes
To serve   6

You will need

2 lb. minced beef
3 oz. breadcrumbs
2 cloves garlic, crushed
2 eggs
salt and pepper
5 tablespoons fat
2 onions, diced
⅖ pint (U.S. 1 cup) soup stock
1 bay leaf (optional)

Mix the beef, breadcrumbs, garlic, eggs, salt and pepper together and form into 6 balls.
Brown in the hot fat and fry the onions in the same fat.
Put the meat balls into a casserole with the fried onion and soup stock. Add the bay leaf.
Roast the meat balls uncovered in a slow oven (275°F. or Gas Mark ½—1) or over low heat for about 45 minutes.

These meat balls are as Jewish as hamburgers are American.

ZEESIH-ZOYIRIH KAHKLEHTEHN

SWEET-SOUR MEAT BALLS

Make as above recipe for kahklehten but use tomato juice instead of soup stock.
Brown sugar and lemon juice (to taste) are often added to the tomato sauce, for sweet-sour kahklehtehn.

Stuffed vine leaves

Cabbage rose salad

SALADS

SALATIM

Except for radish salads, which were popular, Jews of Eastern Europe knew so little of this course that even a tomato was utterly unknown to them. As they moved westward to America and southward to Israel from the Slavic lands, the age-old love of the cucumber was revived and became as popular as it was longed for by our people during the fourty-year desert wanderings with Moses from Egypt to the Holy Land.

Today in Israel salads come with every meal. Sometimes they are Near-Eastern inspired — highly spiced with chillis, dressed with tahina or yoghourt; at times they are rich with mayonnaise and piqued with dill pickles — of Alpine inspiration; they may be fruited with our bountiful citrus — American-style; often they are Balkan-flavoured with sweet peppers and aubergine-bodied; they may be leafy and refreshing with French dressing. Olives and olive oil will turn up as a constant ingredient, as it did in *Erez Israel* from the first. In the kibbutzim—the pioneering settlements with a common kitchen and dining hall — every member makes up his own breakfast salad at table, choosing whatever seasonable vegetables he likes, flavouring with whatever herbs he prefers.

Herbs were so highly favoured in Bible times that they were used as tithes — particularly the dill, mint, anise and cumin. These aromatic delights penetrated, and have been retained, in Jewish cooking of the area: some in meat dishes, many in salads.

RITACHLICH MIT SMETENEH
RADISHES IN SOUR CREAM

No cooking
To serve 6

You will need

20 red radishes
salt to taste
⅖ pint (U.S. 1 cup) sour cream
1 tablespoon sugar
2 tablespoons wine vinegar

Slice and salt the radishes.
Mix the sour cream, sugar and vinegar and stir into the radishes.

This turns up on many Shavuot tables.

PRESSGURKA
CUCUMBER SALAD

No cooking
To serve 6

You will need

6 cucumbers, peeled
1 teaspoon salt
2 tablespoons sugar
1 tablespoon dill, chopped
4 tablespoons mild vinegar
sprinkling caraway seeds (optional)

Thinly slice the peeled cucumbers. Mix with the salt. Place a plate with a weight on it over the cucumbers to squeeze out the liquid. Drain after 1 hour. Mix the remaining ingredients and pour over the cucumbers.

SALAT MILAFAFONIM V'GVINA

CUCUMBER-CHEESE SALAD

No cooking
To serve 8

You will need

8 medium-sized fresh cucumbers
1 spring onion or chives, chopped
12 oz. cottage cheese
scant ¼ pint (U.S. ½ cup) sour cream
7 tablespoons chopped lox (smoked salmon, packed in oil)
salt and white pepper

Slit the cucumbers in two lengthwise. Do not peel them. Scoop out most of the flesh and chop it up coarsely. Add the onion, cheese, sour cream, lox, salt and pepper and mix well. Fill into the cucumber shells and serve chilled on lettuce.

An Israeli summer supper dish.

The Israeli pioneer salad

which the settlers at the communal tables put their eggshells, peels, etc. B'Ta-ahvohn! (Bon appetit!) Every kibbutz settlement in Israel serves this at each meal — including breakfast — where the pioneers dice or slice their own salad concoction at table.

SALAT HAKIBBUTZNIKIM

THE ISRAELI PIONEER SALAD

No cooking

You will need

hard-boiled eggs
olives, black and green
tomatoes
cucumbers
peppers
radishes
onions
kohlrabi
carrots
cabbage
dill, parsley
oil, lemon, vinegar
salt and pepper
sour cream or yoghourt
cottage cheese
garlic

Use what you will, cut as you like, flavour as you wish. Peels go into the 'kol-boynik' (everything into it) — nickname for a bowl at each table in

SALAT KRUVIT

CAULIFLOWER SALAD

Cooking time 10 minutes
To serve 6

You will need

1 medium-sized cauliflower
1¼ pints (U.S. 3 cups) water
1 teaspoon sugar
generous ¼ pint (U.S. ¾ cup) white mild vinegar
3 tablespoons oil
1 teaspoon mustard
salt to taste
dash nutmeg

Break up the cauliflower into fleurets and cook in rapidly boiling water with the sugar and 2 tablespoons of the vinegar. Remove from water when just done (no longer crisp but not too soft) and pour over the remaining ingredients which have been beaten together. Chill and serve with any desired garnish.

A refreshing summer salad.

KARTOFFEL SALAT

POTATO SALAD

No cooking
To serve 6

You will need

2 lb. potatoes, boiled in their skins
  and peeled
2 dill pickles, sliced
3 green onions, chopped
1 large diced sour apple (optional)
salt and pepper
scant ¼ pint (U.S. ½ cup) mayonnaise,
  or more
3 tablespoons vinegar

Dice or slice the potatoes and toss lightly with the pickles, onions and apple. Add salt and pepper. Mix the mayonnaise with the vinegar and pour over. Mix lightly.

German Jews introduced this salad to Israel where it has become a daily summer dish.

SALAT MENTA

MINTED SALAD

No cooking
To serve   6

You will need

4 tomatoes
2 cucumbers
3 red radishes
1 green sweet pepper
1 red sweet pepper (pimento)
3 spring onions, stem and bulb
1 clove garlic, crushed
1 tablespoon chopped parsley
¾ oz. snipped fresh mint
1 small hot pepper (optional)
4 tablespoons olive oil
2 tablespoons lemon juice
salt and pepper

TO GARNISH

pepper top
mint leaves

All vegetables must be uniformly diced into very

Minted salad

small cubes. Chill and serve garnished with a pepper top and mint leaves.

Oriental Jews have loved mint since Bible times, when it was a favourite.

VARIATION

Some Oriental communities pour ⅖ pint (U.S. 1 cup) of yoghourt over this salad.

SALAT LEBEN-KISHUYIM

SQUASH-YOGHOURT SALAD

Cooking time   1 minute
To serve   6

You will need

8 small summer squash or baby marrows
2 tablespoons fresh mint leaves and/or dill
salt and pepper
garlic if desired
generous ½ pint (U.S. 1½ cups) yoghourt

Thinly slice the squash. Add just enough water to half cover the vegetable. Bring to the boil and remove from the heat. Squashes should still be crisp. Drain and chill thoroughly. Gently mix in the herbs, seasoning, garlic if used. Pour on the yoghourt.

VARIATION

Westerners in Israel add 4 tablespoons mayonnaise and 4 tablespoons sour cream to ⅖ pint (U.S. 1 cup) yoghourt.

SALAT PNINEH HA'EMIR

EMIR'S PEARL SALAD

No cooking
To serve   6

You will need

6 oranges, peeled and thinly sliced
2 onions, thinly sliced
18 black olives
olive oil
lemon juice

Slice the oranges and arrange attractively on a plate. Top with circles of sliced onion. Garnish with ripe olives. Sprinkle with olive oil and lemon juice.

TURUHTOE

CUCUMBER SALAD

No cooking
To serve   6

You will need

1 lb. cucumbers
lemon juice
salt
olive oil
dried mint

Slice the cucumbers paper thin or dice into small cubes. Add as much lemon juice as you like. Sprinkle with salt and dress with olive oil and a generous sprinkling of crushed dried mint.

A Sephardic Jewish salad.

SALAT KOHLRAHBI

KOHLRABI SALAD

No cooking
To serve   6

You will need

4 young kohlrabi *
½ teaspoon salt
1 tablespoon lemon juice
2 tablespoons olive oil
1 teaspoon sugar (optional)
black olives for garnish

* The kohlrabi must be young and freshly harvested.

Coarsely grate or very finely slice the kohlrabi. Sprinkle on the salt. Mix the lemon juice with the olive oil and sugar and use as a dressing. Garnish with ripe black olives.

SALAT DAG V'AGVANIYOT

TOMATO AND FISH SALAD

No cooking
To serve   8

You will need

8 medium-sized tomatoes
12 oz. flaked cooked fish
1 tablespoon chopped parsley
4 tablespoons chopped celery stalk or grated celery root
1 tablespoon chopped onion
1 small dill pickle, chopped
2 eggs, chopped
mayonnaise
8 lettuce leaves

Cut the tomatoes into six sections without separating the bottom of the tomato. Spread sections out to form a lily shape. Lightly mix together the fish, parsley, celery, onion, pickle, eggs and mayonnaise

Tomato and fish salad

and pile into the tomato lily. Serve on lettuce leaves.

A summer dish in Israel.

SALAT KRUV-ODOM
RED CABBAGE SALAD

No cooking
To serve　6

You will need

12 oz. shredded red cabbage
2 tablespoons chopped green onion
pinch caraway seeds
dash sugar
dash chopped garlic
4 tablespoons oil
4 tablespoons wine vinegar
salt to taste

Mix all the ingredients together and serve chilled. This salad is equally delicious made with white cabbage.

SALAT LUBIYA
BEAN SALAD

Cooking time　2 hours
To serve　6

You will need

13 oz. navy or other dried beans
salted water to cover
4 cloves garlic, crushed
1—2 red chilli peppers, chopped
scant ¼ pint (U.S. ½ cup) olive oil
juice 2 lemons
½ oz. chopped parsley

Soak the beans overnight. Drain and cover with salted water. Cook for about 2 hours until the skins burst and rise to the top. Remove skins and drain. Add remaining ingredients. Then cool the beans. Serve cold.

A North African salad which is a basic dish in the Moroccan mellah (ghetto) because of its low cost and high flavour.

Bean salad

SALAT YAROK
TOSSED GREEN SALAD

No cooking
To serve　6

You will need

1 clove garlic
1 teaspoon prepared mustard
½ teaspoon salt
dash pepper and paprika
2 teaspoons sugar
4 tablespoons olive oil
juice 1 lemon
2 hard-boiled eggs, chopped
1 large sweet onion
1 large head lettuce
2 tablespoons chopped parsley
1 fleshy sweet green pepper, chopped
3 red radishes, sliced
3 tomatoes, cut into sectors
1 small carrot, finely sliced
2 celery stalks, chopped

Rub a wooden bowl with the garlic. Add the next seven ingredients and mix very well. Put wooden servers into the bowl to keep the dressing from touching the salad until it is mixed. On top of the servers arrange the lettuce leaves in the shape of a head of lettuce, putting layers of all the other vegetables and a sprinkling of the egg and celery in between each layer of lettuce. Mix only at table so salad will be crisp.

SALAT HELYON

ASPARAGUS SALAD

No cooking
To serve   8

You will need

8 lettuce leaves
24 canned asparagus tips (yellow)
16 stuffed green olives
4 hard-boiled eggs, sliced
8 tomato slices
8 slices green peppers
mayonnaise diluted with malt vinegar or
    lemon juice

On the lettuce leaves arrange the asparagus, olives, egg slices and tomato slices. Top with slices of green pepper and garnish with diluted mayonnaise put over the asparagus.

For festive occasions.

REHTACH SALAT

RADISH AND TURNIP SALAD

No cooking
To serve   6

You will need

1 lb. 3 oz. black or red radishes and/or
    turnips
3 tablespoons chopped onions
2 oz. chicken fat or 4 tablespoons olive oil
salt and pepper to taste
18 ripe olives to garnish

Coarsely grate the peeled black radishes and the unpeeled red radishes and, if you wish to bring the high flavour of radishes down, add some turnips. Fry the onions in the chicken fat or olive oil.
Mix with the radish mixture and season to taste. Garnish with ripe olives.

A Russian-Polish Jewish salad, but of ancestry that goes back two millennia when radishes were much loved among the Maccabeans.

Radish and turnip salad

TZING SALAT

TONGUE AND CELERIAC SALAD

No cooking
To serve   6

You will need

1 lb. beef tongue, cooked
1 lb. celeriac or celery root
2 tomatoes
$\frac{2}{5}$ pint (U.S. 1 cup) mayonnaise
1 sweet red pepper
1 tablespoon capers or chopped
    sweet pickles
1 tablespoon olives, chopped
salt and pepper

Cut the cooked beef tongue, celeriac or celery root and tomatoes into julienne (strips of vegetables).
Mix the mayonnaise with the red pepper, capers or chopped sweet pickles and olives. Season with salt and pepper and stir into the meat mixture. Serve on fresh lettuce.

This is an Italian as well as a German-Jewish dish.

Note

You can use chicken in place of tongue in this salad, and use more meat than the above, with equally good results.

SALAT ROUSEE
RUSSIAN SALAD

No cooking
To serve   6

You will need

4 oz. diced cooked potatoes
2 dill pickles, diced
8 oz. diced cooked beetroot
8 oz. cooked peas
8 oz. cooked diced carrots
3 hard-boiled eggs, diced
mayonnaise mixed with sour cream, to taste
salt and pepper

Carefully mix all the ingredients together so they will not get mushy. Serve as a salad or a first course.

At parties Russian old-timers in Israel serve this surrounded with halved egg whites filled with amber and black caviar (the local kosher kind).

SALAT HADARIM V'AVOCADO
AVOCADO-CITRUS SALAD

No cooking
To serve

You will need

1 segmented pomela (optional)
2 segmented grapefruit
3 segmented oranges
2 avocados, cut into wedges
seeds 1 pomegranate
sprinkling lemon juice and sugar
cottage cheese (optional)

Remove membranes from the pomela, grapefruit and orange segments and arrange in a circle with wedges of avocado to alternate the colours. Sprinkle with pomegranate seeds and make a mound of the seeds in the centre. Sprinkle a little lemon juice and then sugar over the fruit. Sometimes a ball of cottage cheese garnished with pomegranate seeds centres the dish.

The most typical of Israel's salad dishes, with the advent of the avocado, the bountiful citrus crops and liking of dairy foods.

Pea-cheese salad

SALAT AFUNAH V'GVINA
PEA-CHEESE SALAD

Mix together 1 can medium-sized peas, 3 oz. finely diced yellow cheese, 7 tablespoons diced sweet pickles, generous $\frac{1}{4}$ pint (U.S. $\frac{3}{4}$ cup) mayonnaise, $\frac{1}{8}$ pint (U.S. $\frac{1}{4}$ cup) liquid from the pickles, salt and pepper to taste. Refrigerate for at least 2 hours so flavours will blend.

This salad is popular in Israel homes of Western origin.

Avocado-citrus salad

SALAT KRUV-SHOSHANA
CABBAGE ROSE SALAD

(Illustrated in colour on page 86)

No cooking
To serve 8—10

You will need

1 large head red cabbage
1 small head white cabbage, shredded
2 grapefruits, skinned and diced
2 apples, diced
4 oz. finely diced celeriac root or
   4 oz. diced celery stalks
scant ¼ pint (U.S. ½ cup) mayonnaise
scant ¼ pint (U.S. ½ cup) sour cream
2 oz. pecans or walnuts or hazelnuts
2 sweet red peppers (pimentos),
   finely slivered

Remove the outside leaves of the red cabbage and cut off the stalk close to the leaves. Fold back the next two layers of leaves and cut out the centre of the cabbage. This shell of red cabbage leaves serves as a rose-petal container for the salad. Put this cabbage shell into cold water for about an hour and then drain it. The remainder of the cabbage is not needed for this salad. Mix the remaining ingredients and fill the shell. Dress if you wish with more mayonnaise and sour cream, garnished with more slivered pimento.

HATZILIM B'PILPEL
AUBERGINE AND PEPPER SALAD

(Illustrated in colour on opposite page)

Cooking time 5—10 minutes
To serve 8

You will need

2 lb. aubergine
juice 1 lemon
3 sweet green peppers
3 sweet red peppers
2 cloves garlic, chopped
2 tablespoons chopped parsley
salt and pepper to taste
scant ¼ pint (U.S. ½ cup) mayonnaise or
   tahina (see page 18)

Put the aubergine over an open flame or under the grill and cook until soft, turning once to roast evenly. Remove the charred skin under running water. Slit the aubergine and let the juice drain off. Break up the aubergine and beat with a wooden spoon, adding the lemon juice as you beat the mixture. Finely chop up the peppers and add with remaining ingredients. Serve in halved peppers.
Rumanian Jews have brought their charred aubergine recipe to Israel where its smoky flavour is much appreciated.

Aubergine and pepper salad

Filled artichoke hearts

VEGETABLES

YIROKOT

'Better a dish of vegetables where love is than rich beef with hatred' declares the Book of Proverbs. It is a quote which came very much alive again with the rebirth of the State of Israel when austerity and rationing were acute in order that refugees could be brought in at a pace that quickly trebled our population with destitute newcomers. Most were survivors of the Nazi concentration camps and families in flight from Arab lands. Though the meat ration dwindled to less than a pound a month there was a pride and reward in subsisting on vegetables with love and aid for our needy brothers.

Israel has a large number of vegetarians because of their sensitivity and respect for the life of any living thing. Many religious Jews over the world turn vegetarian during their travels as the surest and simplest way of maintaining the kosher laws.

Beans, lentils, squash, leeks, garlic, onions, cucumbers were basic vegetables in Bible days and have so remained among Jewish communities in and around the Holy Land. Newcomers to the culinary world (in measures of millennia) such as potatoes, tomatoes, peppers, aubergines (all botanically related) have found their place in Jewish cooking. But dishes like machshi batzal (filled onions), kishuyim mimulayim (stuffed squash), prasah-zeytlinis (leeks and olives) or pul behtarmil (broad beans in pod) seem to stem from timeless source.

HARSHOUF MIMULA
FILLED ARTICHOKE HEARTS

(Illustrated in colour on opposite page)

Cooking time   about 2 hours
To serve   8

You will need

16 artichokes
6 oz. chopped beef
2 tablespoons fine breadcrumbs
1 tablespoon parsley
salt and pepper
2 tablespoons oil
2 eggs
flour
4 teaspoons water
water for cooking
lemon juice to taste

Boil artichokes until tender. Remove the leaves (which can be served separately on another occasion). Remove the choke with a sharp knife in one piece. Fill these little artichoke 'saucer' hearts as follows :

Mix meat with breadcrumbs, parsley, salt and pepper, oil, 1 beaten egg and the seasonings. Fill the artichoke hearts. Roll in flour. Dilute remaining egg with the water and dip the artichokes into this. Fry in hot oil just enough to seal and then put the filled hearts into a casserole, meat side up, and almost cover with water flavoured with lemon juice. Cover and cook over very low heat for about 1½ hours, adding very little water if need be. Just before finishing cooking, add more lemon juice if you like. Serve hot or cold as an appetizer or with fowl. Garnish with egg slices and olives. if you wish.

Sephardic families serve this on Passover, when the vegetable is in season.

HUMTZAH B'ROTEV SEPHARDI

CHICK PEAS IN SPANISH SAUCE

Cooking time   about 2 hours
To serve   6—8

You will need

1 lb. chick peas
water to cover
3 tablespoons oil

SEPHARDIC TOMATO SAUCE

1 sweet green pepper, chopped
1 sweet red pepper, chopped
1 small chilli pepper, chopped
1 onion, chopped
1 clove garlic, chopped
2 tablespoons oil
1 tablespoon parsley, chopped
1 lb. tomatoes, chopped
1 teaspoon salt

To make the sauce lightly fry the peppers, onion and garlic in the oil. Add parsley, tomatoes and seasoning.
Cook on low heat for about 30 minutes, until tomatoes become a pulp.
Soak chick peas overnight. Cover with fresh water and simmer with the oil. When the peas begin to get tender add the tomato sauce and finish cooking.

Chick peas in Spanish sauce

North African Jews make this dish daily.

VARIATION

If you wish, the sauce can be poured on the chick peas just at serving time.

HAG HA'ASIF TZIMMIS

HARVEST FESTIVAL DISH

Cooking time   about 40 minutes
To serve   8

You will need

1 lb. cooked sweet potatoes
1 lb. apples, peeled
1 lb. parboiled pumpkin
salt to taste
2 oz. fat
7 tablespoons honey or orange marmalade
scant ¼ pint (U.S. ½ cup) water
scant ¼ pint (U.S. ½ cup) white wine
juice and grated rind 1 lemon

Thickly slice potatoes, apples and pumpkin and place in alternate layers in a casserole. Mix remaining ingredients and pour over. Bake in a moderate oven (350°F. or Gas Mark 4) for about 40 minutes until apples are done and sweet potatoes glazed.

Served on Succot, symbolic of autumn fruits.

PAZIE

STUFFED STEMS

Cooking time   about 1½ hours
To serve   8

You will need

20 broad stems of either artichoke, celery,
   chard or beet
8 oz. minced meat
2 tablespoons breadcrumbs
1 tablespoon chopped parsley
salt and pepper
1 tablespoon oil
2 eggs
flour
1 tablespoon water
lemon juice to taste
dash cinnamon (optional)

Cut the vegetable stems into 4-inch lengths. Mix
meat with breadcrumbs, parsley, salt, pepper, 1 egg
and seasoning. Fill the stems. Roll in flour. Dilute
remaining egg with the water and dip floured stems
in this. Fry in hot oil just to seal. Put stems into
a casserole, meat side up, and almost cover with
water flavoured with lemon juice. Cover and cook
over low heat for about 1½ hours. Serve hot or cold.

An Old Jerusalem dish, usually served as a first
course.

PRASAH-ZEYTLINIS

LEEKS AND OLIVES

Cooking time   30 minutes
To serve   8

You will need

8 leeks
3 tablespoons olive oil
2 tablespoons margarine
1 tablespoon cornflour
⅖ pint (U.S. 1 cup) chicken stock
2 tablespoons tomato purée
pepper to taste
2 tablespoons sugar
juice 1 lemon
4 oz. large black olives

Cut leeks into strips or rings. Then dip leeks in
boiling water. Drain well, and dry. Fry lightly in

Leeks and olives

the oil. Melt margarine, stir in cornflour and add
the stock. Cook, stirring constantly, until thick.
Add tomato purée, pepper, sugar and lemon juice.
Pour the sauce over the leeks and cook for about
15 minutes until soft. Add the olives at the end and
cook for about 10 minutes. As olives are salty, be
wary of adding more salt.
A dish that perhaps (without tomatoes) dates
back to Bible days when leeks were so loved.

BEBLACH MIT HONIK

BEANS WITH HONEY

Cooking time   about 2½ hours
To serve   6

You will need

14 oz. dried beans
3 onions, diced
2 oz. chicken or other fat
8 tablespoons honey
2 teaspoons salt

Soak beans overnight. Rinse and then cover with
water. Cook over low flame for about 1½ hours until
beans are soft. Drain off the water. Fry the onions
in the fat, then add the honey and salt and mix
with the beans. Bake in a medium oven (350°F. or
Gas Mark 4) for about 1 hour until beans are
glazed.

Some Jewish communities in the Balkans and Near
East have a sweet tooth — even for beans.

KISHUYIM MIMULAYIM
STUFFED SUMMER SQUASH

Cooking time 45 minutes
To serve 6

You will need

18 very small squashes or baby marrows
3 tablespoons oil
2 onions, chopped
1½ lb. tomatoes, chopped
1 teaspoon sugar
1 teaspoon salt
dash chilli pepper
10½ oz. raw rice
1 lb. ground meat
½ teaspoon cinnamon or allspice
1 tablespoon chopped parsley
salt and pepper

Hollow out the unpeeled squashes with an apple corer leaving one end closed. Put most of the pulp into a frying-pan with the oil, onions and tomatoes and fry lightly. Add the sugar, salt and chilli pepper. This tomato mixture will be used as a sauce in which to stew the stuffed squashes. Mix the rice, meat, cinnamon or allspice and parsley with salt and pepper. Half fill the squashes with the meat mixture and seal with a piece of the remaining squash pulp. Put squashes into a pot in layers, with tomato sauce in between. If necessary, add water

Stuffed summer squash

to cover. Simmer, uncovered, very gently for about 35 minutes, until sauce is almost all absorbed and rice cooked.

A Sephardic-Israeli dish of young squashes.

VARIATION

Squashes can be slit lengthwise and hollowed, then filled with above mixture and baked in a shallow pan with the above sauce.

HAZILIM B'AGVANIYOT
AUBERGINES IN ORIENTAL TOMATO SAUCE

Cooking time 45 minutes
To serve 6—8

You will need

2 large aubergines
salt
4 oz. flour
scant ¼ pint (U.S. ½ cup) water
2 eggs, well beaten
oil for frying
pepper
2 cloves garlic, crushed

ORIENTAL SAUCE

1 lb. ripe tomatoes
1 hot chilli pepper
4 teaspoons sugar
½ teaspoon salt
1 clove garlic, crushed

TO MAKE THE SAUCE

Put everything through the mincer and then bring to the boil and cool.
Slice the aubergines with their skins on into ½-inch thick slices. Sprinkle with salt and leave aside to sweat out the moisture. Make a batter of the flour, water and eggs. Dry the aubergine slices, dip in batter and fry in hot oil. Arrange slices in a casserole with a sprinkling of salt and pepper and garlic. Cover with the above sauce or any other tomato sauce (less fiery if you like) and bake in a medium oven (350°F. or Gas Mark 4) for 30 minutes or more. Preferably serve cold. It is also good hot.

The most popular aubergine dish in Israel.

MACHSHI BATZAL
STUFFED ONIONS

Cooking time 1¼ hours
To serve 8

You will need

8 large onions
8 oz. minced beef or lamb
dash allspice
chopped parsley
salt and pepper
2 tablespoons ground almonds (optional)
1 egg
2 tablespoons flour
3 tablespoons oil
juice 1 lemon
water to cover

Cut onions in halves and scoop out the hearts. Chop about 3 tablespoons of the hearts and add to meat with allspice, parsley, salt, pepper, almonds and egg. Fill onions with this mixture. Dust tops of onions with flour and fry them first (meat side down) in the oil. Put remaining onion hearts in another saucepan and add lemon juice and just enough water to cover this onion bed which will act as a steamer. Put filled onions over this bed. Cover saucepan and simmer about 1 hour until onions are soft, adding a little water from time to time.

Served in Sephardic communities as an appetizer, or as a vegetable side dish.

PUL BEHTARMIL
BROAD BEANS IN POD

Cooking time 30—40 minutes
To serve 6

You will need

1 lb. fresh broad beans in pod
4 tablespoons oil
2½ oz. onion
1 clove garlic
1 tablespoon chopped parsley
1 tablespoon chopped fresh dill
salt and pepper to taste
dash nutmeg or cumin (optional)
about ⅖ pint (U.S. 1 cup) water

Chop the onion and wash and string the broad beans. Slice them, pod and bean together. Heat the oil and put in the beans, the chopped onion and the crushed garlic and fry, stirring, for just a minute or two.
Add the remaining ingredients and bring to the boil.
Add only enough water to keep mixture from frying. Cover the saucepan and let the beans cook slowly. Beans are ready in about 30 minutes.

Loved in all the Near East

VARIATIONS

1 You can add any desired tomato sauce towards the end of the cooking.
2 Green string beans can be cooked in this way.

101

ROODE KOOL MET APPELEN
RED CABBAGE WITH APPLES

Cooking time 30 minutes
To serve 6

You will need

1½ oz. margarine
1½ lb. red cabbage, shredded
4 sour apples, peeled and thinly sliced
pinch nutmeg
salt and pepper
⅜ pint (U.S. 1 cup) boiling water
3 tablespoons sugar
3 tablespoons vinegar

In the margarine lightly fry the cabbage and apples, sprinkled with a pinch of nutmeg. Add salt, pepper and the water. Cover the saucepan and cook for about 10 minutes. Add sugar and vinegar; mix well and cook for about another 10 minutes until cabbage is done.

The Dutch version of a dish of many nuances enjoyed by many Jewish communities of Central Europe.

MOUSSAKA
AUBERGINE BAKE

Cooking time about 1¼ hours
To serve 6

You will need

3 medium-sized aubergines
1 teaspoon salt
1 lb. lamb
4 onions, diced finely
3 tablespoons water
2 cloves garlic, minced
6 tablespoons oil
4 tablespoons tomato purée mixed with
  4 tablespoons water
dash pepper
2 tablespoons cornflour
⅜ pint (U.S. 2 cups) broth
4 eggs, slightly beaten

Slice the unpeeled aubergines to ½-inch thickness. Sprinkle with salt and set aside (preferably in the sun) for an hour. Meanwhile mince the lamb, add onions, water and garlic and fry in the oil. Remove from heat and fry the aubergines in the oil until

golden. Mix the tomato purée with the water and a dash of pepper. Put alternate layers of aubergine, meat mixture and tomato purée into a greased casserole, with aubergines as top layer. Bake for 45 minutes in a moderate oven (350°F. or Gas Mark 4). Dissolve cornflour in the broth, add the beaten eggs, mix well and pour on the baked dish. Return to the oven for about 20 minutes until sauce is set. Serve hot.

The Israeli kosher version of the Greek cheese-topped casserole.

BKEILA
CHARD AND BEANS

Cooking time 2½ hours
To serve 6

You will need

8 oz. finely diced head of beef or lamb
  (or other meat)
3 onions, diced finely
2 cloves garlic, chopped
6 tablespoons oil
1 lb. dried beans
salt and pepper to taste
pinch ground coriander
water to cover
1 lb. spinach or Swiss chard

Fry the meat with the onions and garlic in the oil. Add the beans (which have been soaked for a few

Chard and beans

102

hours) and seasoning and just cover with water. After cooking for about 30 minutes, add the chopped spinach or chard. Cover the saucepan and cook on very low heat for about 2 hours until beans are tender and the spinach pulped almost into a sauce.

A Tunisian dish served on Rosh Hashono.

15 minutes until okra is almost soft. Stir in the lemon juice. Cover with the meat balls if you are using meat. Cover the pan and simmer over low heat for about 20 minutes until sauce is thick. Serve hot or cold, preferably with rice.

Served after the Yom Kippur fast in some Sephardic communities.

BAMYA

OKRA IN TOMATO SAUCE

Cooking time   45 minutes
To serve   8

You will need

1 lb. minced meat (optional)
1 clove garlic, chopped (optional)
¼ pint (U.S. ⅔ cup) olive oil or other oil
2 onions, finely chopped
2 lb. young okra
2 lb. tomatoes
2 teaspoons sugar
salt and pepper
juice ½ lemon

If you are using meat mix with garlic and shape into marble-sized balls. Fry in the oil. Remove meat balls and fry the onions in the oil. Remove onions and lightly fry the okra (after cutting the tip off each one). Finely chop the tomatoes and add. Season with sugar, salt and pepper. Cook for about

Okra in tomato sauce

ASPARAGUS POLONI

POLISH STYLE ASPARAGUS

Cooking time   12 minutes
To serve   8

You will need

2 bunches asparagus, trimmed
2 tablespoons breadcrumbs
4 oz. butter
4 hard-boiled egg yolks, chopped
1 tablespoon chopped parsley

Cook asparagus with the tips upwards in rapidly boiling water with 1 teaspoon salt. Drain and put asparagus into a hot serving dish. Sprinkle with breadcrumbs fried in butter and top with chopped egg yolks and parsley.

ZEESIH-KARTOFEL KUGELACH

SWEET POTATO BAKES

Cooking time   30 minutes
To serve   6

You will need

3 tablespoons self-raising flour
1½ lb. mashed sweet potatoes (yams)
2½ oz. chicken fat
3 eggs, beaten
6 oz. brown sugar
⅔ pint (U.S. 1 cup) water
1 teaspoon salt
rind and juice 1 lemon
dash ginger

Mix all ingredients together and whip up well. Two-thirds fill greased deep patty tins. Bake in a moderate oven (350°F. or Gas Mark 4) for about 30 minutes. Serve hot.

NITZANEI-KRUV B'DVASH

BRUSSELS SPROUTS WITH HONEY

Cooking time about 25 minutes
To serve 8

You will need

2 lb. Brussels sprouts
salt to taste
generous ½ pint (U.S. 1½ cups) chicken
soup
12 tablespoons honey
pinch ground cloves (optional)
1 tablespoon lemon juice

Pour boiling water over the Brussels sprouts to blanch them.
Put sprouts into a saucepan, sprinkle with salt to taste and cover with chicken soup. Add honey and cloves and cook for about 15 minutes until the sprouts are tender. Remove sprouts and keep warm. Boil the liquid briskly to reduce so that it can be served as a sauce. Add lemon juice to the sauce, and serve.

A Rosh Hashono dish.

ZEESIH-MAYEHREN

GLAZED CARROTS

(Also illustrated in colour on the jacket)
Cooking time 1½ hours
To serve 6—8

You will need

8 large carrots
orange juice to cover *
4 tablespoons honey or 5½ oz.
sugar
salt to taste
4 tablespoons oil
rind 1 lemon
dash ginger

* Instead of pure orange juice you can use a mixture of orange juice and water.

Cut the carrots into slices and cover with the orange juice. Boil 10 minutes. Add the honey or sugar, salt and oil. Cook gently for about 1 hour until the

Glazed carrots

liquid is almost all absorbed and the carrots slightly glazed. Sprinkle with lemon rind and ginger and cook 15 minutes more.

A Rosh Hashono dish, somewhat different from the traditional carrot tzimmis.

KRUVIT

CAULIFLOWER WITH BUTTERED CRUMBS

Cooking time 20 minutes
To serve 6

You will need

1 large cauliflower
2 pints (U.S. 5 cups) water
2 teaspoons sugar
1 teaspoon salt
2 oz. dry breadcrumbs
8 oz. butter or margarine
dash nutmeg

Divide the cauliflower into fleurets and cook until tender for about 15 minutes with the water and sugar. Drain and sprinkle with salt.
Meanwhile fry the breadcrumbs in the fat over a low heat, stirring constantly. Add the nutmeg. Add the breadcrumbs to the cauliflower (they will cling to the vegetable) and serve hot.

Very popular in Israel.

FUL MEDAMAS

BEANS FROM DAMASCUS

Cooking time 6 or more hours
To serve   6

You will need

14 oz. small brown beans, soaked overnight
2⅔ pints (U.S. 6 cups) water
6 eggs
salt and pepper
3 cloves garlic
3 tablespoons olive oil
16 tablespoons prepared tahina (see page 18)
juice ½ lemon
chopped parsley
pinch turmeric
pinch cayenne, or paprika (if you like
   it less fiery)

Put beans in a large saucepan with eggs in their shells, salt and pepper. When boiling add the garlic and oil and cook in a well-covered saucepan on a very low heat for at least 6 hours (overnight is usual — for it is often prepared for the Sabbath). Serve the beans with the whole shelled eggs next to the tahina mixed with the lemon juice. Garnish the plate with parsley on the tahina, turmeric on the eggs and paprika sprinkled on the beans. Some types of beans, when cooked for so long, have a way of turning purplish and add to the colour of the dish.

KARTOFFEL KUGEL

POTATO BAKE

Cooking time 30 minutes
To serve   6—8

You will need

8 medium-sized potatoes, boiled
1 large onion, chopped
2 oz. chicken fat
3 cracklings, chopped (optional) (page 16)
1 teaspoon salt
pepper to taste
5 eggs

Mash the potatoes. Lightly fry the onion in the chicken fat and add to potatoes and chopped

Potato bake

cracklings with salt and pepper. Separate the egg yolks from the white and beat well, then whip into potatoes. Beat the egg whites until stiff and fold into the potatoes. Bake in a greased casserole in a moderate oven (350°F. or Gas Mark 4) for about 30 minutes, until kugel is golden. Serve at once.

A dish lauded in Yiddish writings for the past two generations.

PAPRIKASBURGONYA

POTATO-PAPRIKA

Cooking time 10—15 minutes
To serve   6

You will need

4 tablespoons oil
3 onions, diced
2 green or red sweet peppers, slivered
8 large potatoes, cooked
⅖ pint (U.S. 1 cup) sour cream
2 teaspoons paprika
salt to taste
sprinkling caraway seeds (optional)

In the oil lightly fry the onions. When they begin to colour, add the peppers. Cube the potatoes, sprinkle with paprika, salt and carraway seeds and fry lightly. Pour on the sour cream, heat through but do not boil, and serve.

TOCH-KARTOFLANIK

POTATO LOAF

(Illustrated on opposite page)

Cooking time   about 1 hour
To serve   6—8

You will need

1 teaspoon sugar
1 oz. fresh yeast
4 tablespoons warm water
1 large onion, chopped
2 tablespoons cooking oil
8 oz. flour, sifted
1 teaspoon salt
pepper to taste
3 eggs, beaten
2 lb. raw potatoes, finely grated

Dissolve the sugar and yeast in the water. Fry the chopped onion in the oil. Sift together dry ingredients.

Mix the yeast with the eggs and add to the fried onion and raw potato. Stir in the flour mixture and knead well on a floured board. Cover with a cloth and set aside in a warm place until almost doubled in bulk. Put into a greased pan and bake in a moderate oven (350°F. or Gas Mark 4) until loaf sets off from sides of pan. Serve hot.
A heavy savoury loaf from Galicia.

TFIHAT KISHUYIM

SQUASH SOUFFLÉ

Cooking time   45 minutes
To serve   6

You will need

5 eggs
8 oz. grated summer squash or vegetable marrow
6 tablespoons sour cream
1 teaspoon prepared mustard
4 tablespoons flour
salt and pepper
4 tablespoons milk
2 tablespoons chopped parsley
1 tablespoon grated onion
1 teaspoon lemon juice

Separate the egg yolks from the whites and beat the yolks into the grated squash. Mix the sour cream, mustard, flour, salt and pepper. Add the milk slowly. Stir in the squash mixture, then the parsley, onion and lemon juice. Beat the egg whites until stiff. Fold the squash mixture in carefully. Pour into a greased casserole and bake in a very moderate oven (300°F. or Gas Mark 2) for 45 minutes. Serve at once.

A typical Israeli dish.

Potato loaf

RELISHES, PICKLES AND GARNISHES

TAVLINIM, CHIBOUSHIM V'KISHUTIM

The spices and spicers mentioned repeatedly in the Bible are coriander, cumin, black cumin, mustard, saffron, cinnamon, rue, garlic, capers, onion, dill and mint. Some of them grow wild in Israel. Though in ancient times most spices were used for medicinal purposes, to make perfume, and some in religious rites, all of them also had their role as condiments. Today they still get into Jewish cooking, particularly pickles.

The wide range of relishes and pickles popular in Israel is evidence of how many different peoples with varied tastes have been ingathered here. The red-hot schoog of the Yemenites requires taste-conditioning for the mustard-loving Westerner who is likely to break out in a sweat at his first hot try.

Marinated peppers of Rumanian origin will be far too flat for an Iraqi Jew who loves chillis. East European Jews stick to dill pickles; Iranians revel in pickled lemons which seem to have a cheesy-fermentation aroma for the Austrian Jew who has to have his Sauerkraut daily. Olives, apparently, are the common denominator of Jewish taste in pickles, for all communities favour it.

The relish that binds all Jewish communities is the religious-inspired chrain — horseradish. It is on Jewish tables on the Passover to symbolize the bitterness we suffered as slaves in Egypt. Because of the cultivated taste for this condiment it has also been adopted non-religiously, to pep up the popular gefilte fish, a dish traditional for the Sabbath.

ZEITIM

HOME CURED OLIVES

(Illustrated in colour on page 113)

GREEN OLIVES

If you hammer the olives they can be cured in a month — otherwise it takes a year.

Soak the olives for three days, changing the water every day. Prepare a brine of 8 oz. coarse salt to every $4\frac{4}{5}$ pints (U.S. 12 cups) water. Pack the olives into jars with any of the following (or combinations) for flavour — garlic, lemon slices, peppercorns, chilli peppers, bay leaves, lemon leaves. Then pour over the brine.

The olives must always be kept under brine or they spoil quickly. Remove the scum and add brine when necessary. After 1 month of fermentation, the olives can be sealed in jars with brine.

BLACK OLIVES

These must be black to the pit. For every $2\frac{1}{4}$ lb. of ripe olives you need 1 lb. coarse salt. Wash and dry the olives. Pack alternate layers of olives and salt in a jar. They are cured and ready to eat after 1 month.

Olives are the mainstay of the Middle Eastern diet.

CHRAIN

HORSERADISH RELISH

No cooking

You will need

12 oz. boiled beetroots
8 tablespoons freshly grated horseradish
scant ¼ pint (U.S. ½ cup) vinegar
1 teaspoon salt
2 tablespoons sugar
pinch pepper

Grate the boiled beetroots. To the grated horseradish, add the vinegar, the salt, sugar and pepper, and the grated boiled beetroots. The beetroots should have been cooked in their skins to retain their colour and flavour.

VARIATION

Sliced dill pickles are often added to this relish before serving.

This relish is always taken with Sabbath gefilte fish and with Passover main dishes.

SAUERKRAUT

PICKLED CABBAGE

(Illustrated in colour on page 113)
No cooking

You will need

1 5-lb. white cabbage
caraway seeds (optional)
coarse salt
water

Finely shred the cabbage. Pack into jars with sprinkling of salt and caraway seeds as you layer the cabbage. Pack in as tightly as possible. Add water to cover and close jars. Add water and a little salt each day as water diminishes. Ready in about a fortnight if kept in a cool place, faster if in a warm room.
Once this was made in barrels, with apples in the cabbage, and during the aromatic fermentation the perfume filled the house.

GARNISHES

These garnishes are really amusing table decorations but could be put with a salad for a buffet party.
To make these figures all you need is a paring knife, scissors, pins, thin nails (to replace pins when fruit is heavy) and a little imagination. The figures are stuck on to flower holders so they stand firmly. For a head choose a fruit that has facial contours such as a lemon, grapefruit, onion, radish, etc. Use spices such as pepper seeds, cloves or vegetables such as peas or bean kernels for eyes. Rings around eyes can be of onion or onion stem. Mouths can be of any red vegetable.
For the body choose a vegetable such as cucumber, squash or potato or even an aubergine. Geranium twigs, rhubarb or celery or many shrubs make bodies. Split a twig to make legs and use branches for arms.
Hair can be made of curly parsley, celery leaves, cauliflower, lettuce, corn stalks etc. Clothing can be made of any leafy vegetable. Pins do most of the fastening.
If a head (like a radish) is too heavy to put on with a pin, pierce the top of the twig with a nail, then insert the nail into the radish head and twist the head of the nail into the twig-head.

Any doll can be made in minutes out of almost any fruit or vegetable. They make good conversation material as well as attractive table decorations.

Jungle girl and old lady

PILPEL HARIF
PICKLED CHILLIS

Cooking time 2 minutes
You will need

⅘ pint (U.S. 2 cups) water
⅘ pint (U.S. 2 cups) vinegar
3½ oz. sugar (optional)
2 teaspoons salt
1 lb. chilli peppers

Bring water, vinegar, sugar, if used, and salt to the boil. Drop in the chillis without cutting the pods. Again bring just to the boil and pack into jars. Ready in one week's time.
All Middle Eastern and Far Eastern Jews dote on this pickle.

LIMONIM HAMOUTZIM
PICKLED LEMONS

(Illustrated in colour on page 113)
Cooking time 20 minutes for sour variety
SWEET

You will need

12 small lemons
3½ lb. sugar
2 tablespoons olive oil

SOUR

12 lemons
3 tablespoons coarse salt
1 tablespoon sweet paprika
3 bay leaves
12 peppercorns
scant ¼ pint (U.S. ½ cup) olive oil

TO MAKE SWEET PICKLED LEMONS
Wash and quarter the unpeeled fruit and pack in a crock with layers of sugar between them. Cover the jar and keep in a cool place until a liquid fills the jar and fermentation begins. Remove the scum and add olive oil. See that lemons remain covered with oil. These will be ready in about 6 months.

TO MAKE SOUR PICKLED LEMONS
Boil the whole fruits for about 20 minutes but do not remove the skin. Drain. Cut each lemon into quarters and layer with the salt and paprika, inserting a bay leaf in the middle and dispersing peppercorns. When the jar is full, pour on the olive

oil. Add more if necessary. Close the jar. The lemons will be ready in about six months.
A quick method is to thinly slice raw lemons and pack into a jar with salt, paprika, bay leaves, peppercorns and set aside for three days. The lemons will exude juice. Add the oil and enough lemon juice to fill the jar. Lemons will be pickled after two weeks.

SCHOOG
HOT YEMENITE RELISH

Cooking time 1 minute
You will need

4 cloves garlic
6 chilli peppers
8 tablespoons chopped fresh coriander
2 cardamom seeds (optional) *
1 tablespoon cumin (optional) *
1 teaspoon salt
2 large tomatoes, chopped
* Use cardamom and cumin only if you cannot get fresh coriander, unless you like everything in it.

Put all the ingredients through the mincer. Bring to the boil. Cool.
This is a chilli sauce so fiery that it takes practice to cultivate a taste for it. Yemenites often dilute it with a Fenugreek Paste called Hilbeh. Some use the sesame paste known as tahina.

Hot Yeminite relish

Zesty beetroot

SELEK MITUBAL
ZESTY BEETROOT

Cooking time   30 minutes

You will need

8 small beetroots
1 teaspoon salt
2 onions, sliced thinly (optional)
2 teaspoons grated horseradish (optional)
$\frac{2}{5}$ pint (U.S. 1 cup) mild vinegar
4 tablespoons sugar
1 bay leaf
6 peppercorns

Cook beetroots in their skins. Then peel and slice them. Put the salt, onions, horseradish, if used, into the vinegar with the sugar, bay leaf and peppercorns. Bring to the boil. Pour this marinade over the beetroots and set aside for a day. They are then ready for use as a pickle or a salad.

LEFET HAMOUTZ
PICKLED TURNIPS

(Illustrated in colour on page 113)
No cooking

You will need

2 lb. small turnips
1 small beetroot
6 tablespoons salt
water, previously boiled and cooled

Peel and quarter the turnips and the beetroot. Pack into a jar and put the salt on top. Pour the cold water on top and close the jar. In two to three weeks time the turnips turn pink and are then ready to eat.

GAMBA V'PILPEL
BETAHMITZ
MARINATED PEPPERS

Cooking time   2 minutes
To serve   8

You will need

16 green and red sweet peppers
salt and pepper
4 tablespoons olive oil
$\frac{2}{5}$ pint (U.S. 1 cup) mild vinegar
pinch garlic (optional)
sugar to taste

Hold each pepper on a fork over an open flame and when it is just charred turn to scorch the other side. Peppers may also be charred under the grill. This charred note adds the necessary flavour. Rinse each pepper after charring in cold water to remove skins. Put them in a bowl, seeds, stem and all. Sprinkle with salt and pepper and pour on the oil. Mix vinegar and garlic, if used, and sugar to taste and pour this on the peppers. After a few hours the peppers are ready.

Marinated peppers

111

AGVANIYOT HAMOUTZOT

PICKLED GREEN TOMATOES

(Illustrated in colour on opposite page)
Cooking time 5 minutes

You will need

20 medium-sized firm green tomatoes
4 oz. salt
generous 2¼ pints (U.S. 6 cups) water
¼ pint (U.S. ⅔ cup) white wine vinegar
4 cloves garlic
3 bay leaves
10 peppercorns
1 teaspoon celery seed
6 whole cloves
3 tablespoons sugar
5 stalks fresh dill or young grape leaves

Wash the tomatoes and pack them into jars. Except the dill, put remaining ingredients into a saucepan and just bring to the boil. Cool the marinade and then pour it over the tomatoes, being sure to cover them. Put dill or grape leaves on top of jars and cover. The tomatoes must be kept covered with the brine at all times. (Once upon a time a plate and a weight was put on pickles in a barrel to keep them covered with brine.) Remove any scum if it appears and if water evaporates, add more water and salt. The pickles are ready to eat in about 1 week.

A West-European Jewish pickle that has become international.

EEGIHRKIS

CUCUMBER DILL PICKLES

(Illustrated in colour on opposite page)
No cooking

You will need

24—30 small cucumbers
3 bay leaves
3 cloves garlic
9 peppercorns
3 stalks fresh dill in seed
3 chilli peppers (optional)
9 tablespoons coarse salt
generous 3½ pints (U.S. 9 cups) water
3 tablespoons vinegar (optional)

Wash the cucumbers and pack them into three 2-pint jars. Top each jar with a bay leaf, a clove of garlic, 3 peppercorns, 1 dill stalk and, if desired, 1 small chilli pepper. Mix water, salt and vinegar and bring to the boil. Cool and then pour over the cucumbers. Be sure that cucumbers and spices remain under water, adding more water and salt if it evaporates. Remove any scum if it appears. If you make this in a crock, put a plate and weight on top to keep the cucumbers under the brine. When cucumbers turn from green to yellow and then olive green they are ready to eat — a week in warm climates, a fortnight in cooler ones.

This awakens more nostalgia for Grandma's cooking than any other pickle.

A selection of pickles

Grape and melon cup

DESSERTS

KINOUCHE I SEUDAH

Desserts in Jewish cuisine fall mainly into two categories: the rich heavy kugels and shalets served for the Sabbath meal in the Diaspora, and the fragrant fruit dishes so refreshing in the warm climate of Israel.

As kindling a fire is prohibited on the Sabbath (a law that pre-dates electric switches and goes back to the time when it was indeed a chore), hot desserts are put to bake from Friday sundown, just before the Rest Day begins, and stay in the oven until Saturday lunchtime. The long baking on a very low heat mellows these dishes to a delight beyond imagination.

Fruit dishes in Israel are many, for new crops are harvested all year round. Citrus crops produce the succulent Jaffa orange and luscious grapefruit,

as does every fruit of this family's trees. The result is that citrus is the base of most of Israel's fruit cups.

The Bible reads like a botanical guide book of Israel's thriving orchards today. Even the watch-towers of the vineyards mentioned in Isaiah 5:2 are part of the harvest-time landscape in modern Israel. Besides the apple, apricot, carob, citron, dates, figs, melons, mulberries, olives and nuts written about in The Book, the recipe for grape-melon cup reads as if the fruits were from the garden of King Solomon — who so hospitably invited his love to enter and eat of its pleasant fruits. It is made of the fruits of the vine, the much-loved beautiful pomegranates, fragrant with mint, and also dressed with honey which Solomon adored.

POODINK TAPUZIM

ORANGE PUDDING

(Illustrated in colour on page 123 and on the jacket)

Cooking time   about 10 minutes
To serve   6

You will need

4½ oz. sugar
5 tablespoons cornflour
pinch salt
1¼ pints (U S. 3 cups) orange juice
3 eggs
2 teaspoons lemon juice

Mix the sugar, cornflour and salt. Heat the orange juice and stir in the dry ingredients. Cook in a double saucepan until mixture is thick. Stir often. Remove from heat. Separate the egg yolks from the whites; beat the egg yolks and add a little of the hot custard to them, stirring well. Put egg mixture into remaining custard and cook over hot water for 2 minutes more, stirring all the while. Then add the lemon juice. Beat the egg whites until stiff and fold into the custard mixture. Pour into individual glasses. Serve chilled.

Cornflour puddings are popular in Israel and made like blancmange. This one is enriched and fluffed with eggs.

MILCHIDIKI LOKSHEN KUGEL

DAIRY NOODLE BAKE

Cooking time   40 minutes
To serve   6

You will need

1 lb. noodles (medium width)
1 pint (U.S. 2½ cups) boiling water
2 oz. butter
⅘ pint (U.S. 2 cups) milk
2 eggs, well beaten
4 oz. sugar
1 teaspoon salt
6 tablespoons raisins
1 teaspoon vanilla
dash ginger (optional)

Parboil the noodles in the boiling water, then drain but do not rinse. Mix all remaining ingredients and stir in the noodles. Bake in a well-buttered shallow casserole in a moderate oven (350°F. or Gas Mark 4) for about 30 minutes or until done.

A dairy dish of the Shavuot festival.

APFELSHALET

DEEP APPLE PUDDING

Cooking time   1 hour or more
To serve   8

You will need

PASTRY

12 oz. flour, sifted
8 oz. margarine or suet
4 tablespoons sugar
rind and juice 1 lemon
2 egg yolks
4 tablespoons water

FILLING

3 lb. apples
7 oz. brown sugar
1 teaspoon cinnamon
dash cloves
peel and juice 1 lemon
3 oz. raisins
2 tablespoons flour

Deep apple pudding

Mix all ingredients for the pastry and roll out. Cover sides and bottom of a casserole with the pastry. Peel apples and cut into sections. Dust with sugar, cinnamon and cloves and sprinkle with rind and lemon juice. Wash raisins and roll in flour, then add to the filling mixture. Put in the fruit and cover with remaining pastry dough. Prick with a fork. Dab top generously with margarine. Bake in a moderate oven (350°F. or Gas Mark 4) for about 1 hour. Sprinkle top crust with white sugar just as you take the dish out of the oven.
This dish can be baked overnight for the Sabbath, or as above. If baked overnight do so in a very slow oven (200°F. or. Gas Mark 0—½) and cover pastry with foil after 1 hour of baking.

PAREVE GLIDAH

NON-CREAM ICE-CREAM

Cooking time   3 minutes
To serve   24

You will need

1 lb. 7 oz. margarine
generous 1¼ pints (U.S. 3¼ cups) water
10 egg yolks
7 oz. sugar
14 oz. chopped nuts (optional)
9 oz. baking chocolate, melted
1 medium-sized egg

Put the margarine in a blender, adding the water gradually until it is light and fluffy. Separately in the blender whip the egg yolks and gradually beat

Non-cream ice cream

Stewed prunes

in the sugar. After a few seconds add nuts and chocolate. Put the yolk mixture in top of double saucepan and cook, whipping constantly for 3 minutes. Do not allow it to boil. Remove from heat and add to the margarine mixture in the blender. Add the whole egg and blend for ½ minute more. Put into the freezer at lowest setting and freeze without stirring. Precision is vital in making this dish. If you put this into 4 trays it will serve 24.

This can be eaten at kosher meat meals, though it tastes like real cream ice-cream.

FLOHMEN COMPOTE
STEWED PRUNES

Cooking time 30 minutes
To serve 8

You will need

8 oz. dried apple rings
8 oz. prunes
generous 1½ pints (U.S. 4 cups) water
8 tablespoons sugar (more if you wish)
1 lemon, cut in two
4 tablespoons blanched almonds or
  prune kernels (optional)

Soak the apple rings and prunes for a few hours in the water. Add the honey and the lemon and cook very gently for about 30 minutes until apples and prunes are soft. Add the blanched nuts just before the compote is finished. Remove the lemon. The rind gives the compote a wonderful nuance of flavour. Cool. Serve cold.

A regular Sabbath dessert.

COUSCOUS IM PEYROT
FRUITED COUSCOUS

Cooking time about 45 minutes
To serve 10

You will need

½ teaspoon salt
⅖ pint (U.S. 1 cup) boiling water
1 lb. coarse semolina
20 pitted dates
20 almonds
7 oz. nuts
grated rind 2 oranges
6 oz. raisins
3½ oz. sugar
4 tablespoons olive oil
juice 1 orange
2 teaspoons Arak or Curaçao
4 tablespoons currants

Add the salt to the boiling water and pour over the semolina. Stir in one direction.

Place semolina in a sieve over rapidly boiling water and steam for 30 minutes, stirring twice. Fill the dates with the almonds and put on top of the semolina to soften. Meanwhile grind or pound together the nuts, orange rind and raisins and add sugar and olive oil. Add orange juice and flavouring. When couscous forms into little grain bundles it is cooked. Remove the dates.

Fold in the ground fruits and form into a pyramid. Garnish with the stuffed dates and the currants. Moroccan Jews eat this on Tu'Bshvat.

FLUDEN
LAYERED BAKED PUDDING

Cooking time   1½ hours
To serve   8

You will need

PASTRY

1 lb. flour
3 teaspoons baking powder
7 oz. sugar
3 tablespoons cooking oil
2 eggs, beaten
4 tablespoons water

FILLING

7 oz. sugar
1 teaspoon cinnamon
7 oz. chopped nuts
8 tablespoons apricot jam
4 oz. shredded coconut (or cut-up
     Turkish delight)
3 oz. raisins and/or chopped dates
3 apples, sliced
sugar and spice for topping

To make the pastry sift the flour, baking powder and sugar. Add oil, eggs and water and mix. Divide the dough into five parts, one a little larger than the others. Roll out as thinly as possible. Place largest piece in a buttered baking dish, covering

Layered baked pudding

sides and bottom. Mix the filling ingredients. Spread one fourth of the filling ingredients on the dough. Fit in next piece of dough and proceed with layering until all ingredients are used up. Top should be of pastry. Sprinkle top with a little more sugar and spice and bake in a very moderate oven (300°F. or Gas Mark 2) for 1½ hours.

Note

You can use other fresh and dried fruits and nuts, and if you like you can put a different fruit on each layer.

VARIATION

Dough can be thickly divided in two, with only one filling.

On Simhat Torah fluden is served with white blossoms on the plate, for purity symbolism.

MERGTAART
MARROW TART

Cooking time   1 hour
To serve   8

You will need

PASTRY

8 oz. flour, sifted
8 oz. margarine or chopped suet
5¼ oz. sugar
½ teaspoon salt
3 teaspoons water

FILLING

2 rusks
12 tablespoons beef marrow
3½ oz. sugar
1 teaspoon mixed cinnamon, allspice, cloves
6½ oz. ground almonds
3¾ oz. candied peel or chopped dried fruits
4 eggs, separated

To make the pastry mix all ingredients together and line a casserole with two-thirds of the rolled dough. Grate the rusks and sprinkle half on the pastry. Melt the marrow and add the sugar, spices, ground almonds, fruits, beaten egg yolks and remaining rusk crumbs. Beat the egg whites until stiff and fold into the mixture. Pour this over the pastry. Roll out remaining pastry, cut into strips and lattice the top of the filling. Bake in a moderately hot oven

(375°F. or Gas Mark 5) for about 1 hour and serve warm.
A hot Dutch dish suitable for dinner in the chilly tabernacle on Succot.

SABRA COMPOTE
PRICKLY PEAR DESSERT

Cooking time   4 minutes
To serve   8

You will need

7 oz. sugar (or more, to taste)
generous 1½ pints (U.S. 4 cups) boiling water
16 whole sabras (prickly pears), peeled *
juice 1 lemon

* Red raspberries and red or purple plums together, substitute for the look and something of the taste of the sabras.

Add the sugar to the boiling water, and when it bubbles add the fruit. Cook for no more than 3 minutes. Remove from heat and add lemon juice.

Note

Sabras are delightful raw, served with a sprinkling of lemon juice and powdered sugar, and garnished with strawberries.
Native Israelis are called 'sabras' because like the prickly pear (fruit of the cactus) they are brusquely thorny on the outside but tenderly sweet within.

Prickly pear dessert

Baked pear pudding

BAHRIN SHALET
BAKED PEAR PUDDING

Cooking time   3½ hours
To serve   6

You will need

3 tablespoons cooking oil
1 lb. flour, sifted
2 eggs
4 tablespoons breadcrumbs
7 oz. sugar
pinch salt
generous ¼ pint (U.S. ¾ cup) water
4 oz. suet or margarine

FILLING

6 large pears
sugar and cinnamon to taste
red wine to cover

Mix pastry ingredients and roll out to ½ inch thickness. Put the oil in a deep casserole, fit in the dough around the wall of the dish and bake in a moderately hot oven (375°F. or Gas Mark 5) for 20 minutes. Meanwhile quarter the pears and cook them with the sugar and the cinnamon in just enough wine to cover. When the pastry is almost done, moisten it with the pear sauce and fill in with the fruit. Bake in a very slow oven (225°F. or Gas Mark 0—¼) for about 3 hours. Serve this dish warm.

An old Jewish-Alsatian recipe.

Apple pudding with wheat

APFEL KUGEL MET WAATZ
APPLE PUDDING WITH WHEAT

Cooking time   4 hours
To serve   8

You will need

3 lb. apples
10½ oz. sugar
2 teaspoons cinnamon
dash cloves and allspice
¼ teaspoon salt
1 tablespoon grated lemon peel
12 oz. flour
6 oz. raisins
7 oz. chopped dates
2 oz. preserved ginger, cut up
6½ oz. almonds
10½ oz. chopped suet or margarine
generous ½ pint (U.S. 1½ cups) lukewarm
   water
4 tablespoons cracked wheat (if unavailable,
   use pearl barley)
red wine (optional)

Peel and cut apples into thin slices. Line a deep
casserole with the fruit fitted into a pattern.
Sprinkle with 5¼ oz. sugar, half the cinnamon and
the other spice, salt and lemon peel. Sift flour over
raisins and chopped dates. Add ginger, remaining
sugar, cinnamon, salt and lemon peel; add the nuts
and suet or margarine. Put mixture into the nest
of apples and seal up with a covering of more apple
slices fitted closely together. Pour the warm water

around the edge of the pudding until entirely
covered. Sprinkle the wheat over the top. Cover
and simmer for about 2 hours adding more water
or wine if necessary. Then put into a slow oven
(250°F. or Gas Mark ¼—½) and bake for 2 hours
more. Add water or wine from time to time as the
pudding must stew. This dish improves with keep-
ing for a week and can be reheated.

The Dutch pudding of Shabbat **Beshalach**.

ASHKALIT B'GRILL
GRILLED GRAPEFRUIT

Cooking time   15 minutes
To serve   6

You will need

3 grapefruit
1½ oz. butter
6 tablespoons sugar or honey
6 cherries and mint sprigs (optional)
6 teaspoons warm brandy
6 cubes sugar (optional)

Cut grapefruit in half, and loosen each section from
the skin and membranes. Fill the core with butter
and sprinkle the sugar or honey well over the fruit.
Grill for 15 minutes, about 3 inches from low heat.
Serve hot, garnished with a cherry and a sprig of
mint in the core. If you like, pour a teaspoon of

Grilled grapefruit

warm brandy over a cube of sugar on each hot grapefruit before serving, and set alight.

An Israeli dessert that can also be an hors-d'oeuvre or served at breakfast.

Note

If you put the sugar on well ahead of time you get a sweeter dessert, but you will have to add more just before grilling.

TAMARIM V'OREZ B'MAI SHOSHANIM

DATE AND RICE ROSE PUDDING

Cooking time   40 minutes
To serve   12

You will need

2 eggs
⅞ pint (U.S. 2 cups) milk
1 lb. cooked rice
7 oz. chopped dates
2 oz. sugar (more if you wish)
2 oz. butter
1 teaspoon rose water (vanilla if you wish)
rose petal or strawberry jam for sauce
rose blooms for garnish (optional)

Date and rice rose pudding

Beat the eggs with a rotary beater and stir in the milk, the cooked rice, chopped dates, sugar, butter and the rose water.
Bake in a moderate oven (350°F. or Gas Mark 4) for 40 minutes. Cool and then chill.
Serve with a sauce of rose petal or strawberry jam.

If you like the pudding can also be garnished with a full-blown red rose for symbolism and beauty. *Tamarin v'orez b'mai shoshanim* is a Persian dish of Shavuot.

This is the festival the Persians call 'Feast of the Roses'.

SHABBAS-KEEGIL

SABBATH BREAD PUDDING

Cooking time   overnight
To serve   6

You will need

2 eggs
12 oz. fresh fruit
10 slices white bread
8 oz. chicken fat
1½ oz. sugar
rind and juice 1 lemon
1 teaspoon cinnamon
¼ teaspoon mixed allspice, nutmeg, ginger
½ teaspoon salt
2 tablespoons water
fat for topping

Beat the eggs and dice the fresh fruit.
Soak the slices of white bread in water, squeeze out the moisture and crumble up.
Mix with the chicken fat, sugar, eggs, lemon rind and juice, cinnamon, allspice, nutmeg, ginger, salt, water and fresh fruit if used.
Put the mixture into a greased heavy ovenproof dish or casserole. Dot with bits of fat on top. Cover and bake in a very slow oven (225°F. or Gas Mark 0—¼) from sundown on Friday night until lunch on Sabbath.
Keegil will be warm, crusty on the outside and soft within.

This is a very ancient dish.

KOS-ANAVIM V'MILON

GRAPE AND MELON CUP

(Illustrated in colour on page 114)
No cooking
To serve   8

You will need

1 lb. green grapes
1 lb. honeydew melon balls
1 lb. watermelon balls
1 lb. purple grapes
6 tablespoons honey
6 tablespoons lemon juice
2 tablespoons pomegranate seeds
mint sprigs

Mix all the fruit balls together.
Dress with honey mixed with lemon juice and garnish with pomegranate seeds and mint sprigs. Put a few leaves of the mint into the fruit mix for taste and smell. Serve chilled in sherbet glasses.

An Israeli summer dessert.

HAFTA'AHT SOLET

SEMOLINA SURPRISE

Cooking time   3 minutes
To serve   6

You will need

generous ½ pint (U.S. 1½ cups) water
generous ½ pint (U.S. 1½ cups) orange juice
6 oz. semolina
grated rind 3 lemons
7 oz. sugar
scant ¼ pint (U.S. ½ cup) lemon juice

Boil the water. Mix the orange juice with the semolina and add to boiling water. Stir and bring just to the boil. Put into the electric mixer; add remaining ingredients and whip until mixture has cooled. Serve chilled in glasses.

A refreshing Israeli dessert.

MIKZEFET LIMON

LEMON WHIP

(Illustrated in colour on opposite page)
No cooking
To serve   8

You will need

8 eggs, separated
8½ oz. sugar
1 package lemon jelly powder
   (sugared-flavoured gelatine)
scant ¼ pint (U.S. ½ cup) boiling water
scant ¼ pint (U.S. ½ cup) heated lemon juice
1 teaspoon grated lemon rind

Beat the egg yolks until thick and pale. Gradually add the sugar and continue to beat. Dissolve the jelly powder in the boiling water and hot lemon juice and beat into the yolks. Add the grated lemon rind. Cool this mixture and then set to chill until it just begins to thicken. Beat egg whites until stiff. Whip up the yolk mixture and fold it into the whites.
Pour into dessert glasses and leave to set. Serve cold.

Israel's boom-boon of citrus and egg production has put this dish into its national cuisine.

Lemon whip; orange pudding

Honey cake; Sabbath sponge cake

CAKES AND BISCUITS

UGOT V'UGIYOT

The first recorded pastry in history is when our Patriarch Abraham ordered our Matriarch Sarah to bake a cake, giving her not only the measures for the recipe, but how to prepare it, also telling her about the stove, and the timing! (See Genesis 18:6.) All kinds of cakes seem to have been baked from then on in Bible days: wafers made with honey (Exodus 16:31) must have been something like the honey-saturated Sarah-Leah pastries in Israel even today. Or perhaps they were the Zelebi-Zingolas of Middle Eastern Jews, for the exact preparation of them — spiral-shaped and honey-dipped — is shown in detail on a tomb painting of Rameses III. In the book of Samuel I we are introduced to fruit cakes of figs — so good that Abigail took two hundred of them to David!

Then came the day when crisp biscuits — cracknels — Kings I, 14:3 were taken by Jeroboam's wife to the house of Ahijah. What good wife today wouldn't take crisp mandelbrodt or mohn platzhen on a call?

Further in our history we adopted cooking ideas from the pagan folk around us: Jeremiah the Prophet inveighed against our women for making cakes shaped into moon crescents for Astarte, the Queen of Heaven! Would he be angry today to see the Jewish housewife knead dough as they did then, in crescent shapes, for the Austrian mohn kipfel?

UGAT GVINA

COTTAGE CHEESE CAKE

(Illustrated in colour on page 133)

Cooking time 1 hour

You will need

5 eggs, separated
7 oz. sugar
1 tablespoon flour
1 tablespoon semolina
1 lb. cottage cheese, sieved
scant $\frac{1}{4}$ pint (U.S. $\frac{1}{2}$ cup) sour cream
grated rind 1 lemon
1 teaspoon vanilla
6 tablespoons white raisins (optional)
6 tablespoons biscuit or cracker crumbs

Cream the egg yolks and sugar until light.
Add the flour, semolina, sieved cheese and cream and mix well.
Add the lemon rind, vanilla and raisins and continue to mix.
Beat egg whites until stiff and fold in.
Butter a baking tin and sprinkle on the crumbs. Spoon on the mixture and bake in a moderately hot oven (375°F. or Gas Mark 5) for about 45 minutes, then turn off the oven and let the cake cool in it for another 15 minutes.
It is best not to open the oven while this cake bakes.

A typical Shavuot cake.

KUBANEH

YEMENITE YEAST CAKE

Cooking time 1½ hour (or overnight for Sabbath)

You will need

7 oz. jam (any kind)
7 oz. sugar (or less)
1½ oz. fresh yeast
⅖ pint (U.S. 1 cup) lukewarm water
6 tablespoons melted butter
⅖ pint (U.S. 1 cup) milk or water
14 oz. flour
pinch salt and ginger
16 tablespoons melted margarine

Mix the jam, sugar and yeast in the water and set aside for a few minutes. Add the melted butter and milk. Sift flour into the mixture, add ginger and salt and stir well. Set aside to rise, covered with a cloth, for 1½ hours. Put 8 tablespoons melted margarine into a heavy saucepan or a tube pan. Pour in the batter. Top with remaining margarine. Set aside for 30 minutes more to rise. Cover the saucepan and bake overnight in a very slow oven (200°F. or Gas Mark 0). Serve warm, with plenty of butter. Or, if you prefer, bake at 350°F. or Gas Mark 4 for about 1½ hours.

When this cake is baked overnight it is much like a kugel. Served warm on Sabbath, with melted butter.

Yemenite yeast cake

Note

Yemenites use only 1 tablespoon of sugar, but the recipe in Israel has sweetened as their lives grew better.

UGIYOT SARA-LEA

SARAH-LEAH PASTRY

Cooking time about 1 hour
To make 5 pastries

You will need

1 recipe filo pastry (see almond strudel, page 129)
4 oz. melted butter
5 oz. cake or biscuit crumbs
4 oz. chopped walnuts, hazelnuts or pecans
½ teaspoon cinnamon
grated rind 1 lemon
8 oz. honey
⅖ pint (U.S. 1 cup) water
1 teaspoon vanilla

Divide the stretched dough into 10 sheets and use two at a time — one over the other. Brush with melted butter. Put cake crumbs over one-eighth of the dough nearest to you. Fold over the edges. Sprinkle on the nuts, cinnamon and lemon rind. Roll up over a metal knitting needle, then squeeze together like an accordion and remove the needle. Bake in a slow oven (250°F. or Gas Mark ½) for about 1 hour, until golden. Bring honey and water to the boil. Pour the honey over the pastry as soon as it comes out of the oven.

Served on Rosh Hashono by Mediterranean communities. Western tastes require each pastry to be cut into five pieces as they are so rich.

BAKLAVA

TURKISH-GREEK PASTRY

Cooking time about 45 minutes
To make 24 pieces

You will need

1 recipe filo dough (see almond strudel, page 129)
1¼ lb. butter or margarine
12 oz. walnuts
14 oz. sugar
generous ¼ pint (U.S. ⅜ cup) water
lemon juice as desired

Turkish-Greek pastry

Poppyseed cake

Cut the filo dough to fit your deep baking tin. Place two sheets on at a time, brush with butter, and sprinkle a few nuts here and there. You will need about 12 or more sheets for each baking tin. Sprinkle on more nuts as you near the top. Cut into rhomboid serving pieces and bake in a moderate oven (350°F. or Gas Mark 4) for about 45 minutes until golden. Drain off the excessive fat twice during the baking. Prepare a syrup of the sugar, water and lemon juice. Spoon this syrup over the pastry immediately after removing from the oven and draining off the fat. After it has cooled you can remove the baklava. Very sweet and rich, but so popular among East Mediterranean Jewish communities that it is served on every festival.

MOHN TORTE

POPPYSEED CAKE

Cooking time   1 hour 20 minutes

You will need

11¼ oz. fine white sugar
7 oz. ground poppyseeds
1 tablespoon rum
⅖ pint (U.S. 1 cup) milk
6 eggs, separated
butter
about 2 oz. flour
sweetened whipped cream (optional)

Mix together 4½ oz. sugar with the poppyseeds, rum and milk and cook over a low heat, or better still in a double saucepan, stirring often, for 20

minutes. Cool. Mix egg yolks with 3½ oz. sugar and cream together well, then gradually add the yolk mixture to the poppyseed mixture. Beat the egg whites until stiff and whip in remaining sugar. Fold the two mixtures together.

Spread some butter rather thickly on to a deep pie dish and sprinkle on the flour until the butter is hidden. Carefully spoon on the cake mixture and bake in a moderate oven (350°F. or Gas Mark 4) for about 1 hour. Serve, if you wish, with a topping of sweetened whipped cream.

GUGELHUPF

YEAST CAKE

Cooking time   50 minutes

You will need

1 oz. fresh yeast
⅖ pint (U.S. 1 cup) warm milk
⅖ pint (U.S. 1 cup) melted margarine
3½ oz. sugar
5 eggs
scant ¼ pint (U.S. ½ cup) orange juice
14 oz. flour

Put yeast into milk; set aside for about 20 minutes. Cream fat and sugar; whip in one egg at a time. Add juice and mix well. Beat in yeast mixture. Add flour to yeast mixture. Set aside, covered, to rise (until double in bulk) in a warm place. Bake for about 50 minutes at 350°F. or Gas Mark 4.

APFEL SHTRUDEL
APPLE STRUDEL

Cooking time   55 minutes

You will need

GRANDMA'S STRETCHED DOUGH

10 oz. flour
1 teaspoon salt
2 tablespoons oil
2 eggs
¼ pint (U.S. ⅔ cup) lukewarm water

FILLING

2½ lb. sliced apples
1½ oz. margarine
7 oz. sugar
4 tablespoons raisins
4 tablespoons chopped almonds
rind 1 orange and 1 lemon
cinnamon and allspice
sugar for sprinkling

To make the dough mix the flour, salt, oil, eggs and water. Knead very well and beat with a rolling pin and pick up the dough and lash it against the table. Let dough rest for 10 minutes in a warm place. Cover a round table with a cloth and dust with flour. Roll dough out as thinly as possible. Put it into the centre of the table and then stretch it on the back of your hands until it is almost paper thin. Sprinkle the dough with the melted margarine and cover with the fruit and remaining ingredients. Roll up the dough by lifting the cloth underneath it. Bake in a very hot oven (450°F. or Gas Mark 8) for

10 minutes, then reduce heat to 350°F. or Gas Mark 4, and bake for a further 45 minutes. Sprinkle with sugar as you remove strudel from oven.

Note

There are many strudel doughs — the strudels here are each given with a different pastry to show the variety. All of them are of thin dough, rolled up to hold a fruit or other filling.

SHTRUDEL PEYROT YIVEHSHIM
DRIED FRUIT STRUDEL

Cooking time   35 minutes

You will need

NOODLE DOUGH*

2 eggs
pinch salt
4 tablespoons oil
2 tablespoons sugar
½ pint (U.S. 1¼ cups)water
12 oz. flour

FILLING

6 tablespoons or more melted margarine
6 tablespoons or more sugar
6 tablespoons shredded coconut
6 tablespoons raisins
6 tablespoons almonds, coarsely chopped
6 tablespoons chopped dates
6 tablespoons candied cherries
6 tablespoons cut-up Turkish delight
(optional)
6 tablespoons cake crumbs
grated rind 1 lemon

* Other strudel doughs can be used.

To make the dough lightly beat the eggs, add the salt, oil, sugar and the water, then work in the flour to make a dough. Knead well. On a floured board, roll dough out as thinly and evenly as possible. Brush the dough with the melted margarine, sprinkle on all the remaining ingredients and then roll up. Put on to a baking tin and cut the pieces without separating them. Brush with more melted margarine. Bake in a moderate oven (375°F. or Gas Mark 5) for about 35 minutes. As soon as the strudel has cooled sprinkle it generously with icing sugar. This keeps very well for weeks.

MANDLEN SHTRUDEL
ALMOND STRUDEL

Cooking time   30 minutes

You will need

THE FILO DOUGH*

11 oz. flour
½ pint (U.S. 1¼ cups) water
1 tablespoon salt

* The dough of this pastry is known as *yufka* in Turkey and *filo* in Greece. It is so thin you can mistake it for paper.

THE FILLING

6 tablespoons melted margarine
13 oz. blanched almonds, chopped
5 egg yolks, beaten
7 oz. sugar
grated rind 1 lemon

To make the pastry mix all ingredients and knead until it is smooth. Put dough aside to rest for 1 hour. Then proceed to roll and stretch as for 'grandma's dough' in recipe for apple strudel (see page 128). When dough is paper thin brush it with melted margarine.
Mix the almonds with the egg yolks, sugar and rind and spread over half the dough. Roll up and brush the top with more melted margarine. Bake in a moderately hot oven (375°F. or Gas Mark 5) for about 30 minutes until golden on top.

MAMOUL
FILLED SEMOLINA CAKES

Cooking time   25 minutes
To make   20 mamouls

You will need

THE DOUGH

1 lb. 3 oz. semolina
2 oz. flour
⅜ pint (1 U.S. cup) oil or melted
   margarine
7 oz. sugar

THE FILLING

5 oz. walnuts, finely chopped
dash cinnamon
4 oz. sugar
1 teaspoon rose essence or vanilla essence
icing sugar for sprinkling

Filled semolina cakes

To make the dough mix all ingredients together and set aside for about 1 hour. Form into oval cakes. For the filling mix all ingredients together. Insert thumb into each cake to make a pocket for filling, put in filling and then close up.
Trim the tops of the cakes with a fork into any marked pattern. Bake for 25 minutes in a moderate oven (350°F. or Gas Mark 4). When cool, sprinkle generously with icing sugar.

OZNEI HAMAN
HAMAN'S EARS

Cooking time   about 3 minutes
To make   25 pastries

You will need

2 eggs
8 oz. flour, sifted
1 teaspoon baking powder
pinch salt
warm water
oil for deep frying
icing sugar

Mix the eggs, flour, baking powder and salt. Add just enough warm water to make a dough that can be rolled. Roll thinly and cut into strips. Fry in deep hot oil and twirl the dough a bit to shape into odd ear shapes. Drain and sprinkle with icing sugar. This pastry varies slightly in different countries where Jewish communities make it on Purim. Names sound different — like the hamansooren of Holland or orecchie de Aman in Italy.

HAMANTASCHEN M'BAZEK PARIKH
CRISP HAMAN'S POCKETS

Cooking time   25 minutes
To make   28 pastries

You will need

THE PASTRY

8 oz. flour, sifted
2 teaspoons baking powder
3½ oz. sugar
pinch salt
2 eggs, well beaten
6 tablespoons oil
grated rind 1 lemon

POPPYSEED FILLING

1 lb. poppyseeds
4 tablespoons honey
1 egg
1 tablespoon lemon juice
4 tablespoons chopped nuts

To make the pastry sift the dry ingredients. Add the eggs, oil and lemon rind. Mix well and roll out thinly on a floured board. Cut into rounds. To make the filling, wash the poppyseeds in hot water, strain and, if not already ground, put through the mincer. Mix with the honey and cook over very low heat for 5 minutes. Remove from heat and add remaining ingredients. Cool. Place a spoonful of filling on each round and bring edges together into triangles. Pinch edges together. Bake in a moderately hot oven (375°F. or Gas Mark 5) for about 20 minutes.

This type of cake keeps well for weeks.

Note

Traditionally, pastry is cut into rounds and sealed by bringing three folds together and pinching edges together, but leaving a small space open for filling to show on top.

MOHN STRUDEL
POPPYSEED YEAST ROLL

Cooking time   1 hour

You will need

1 recipe gugelhupf yeast cake (see page 127), without topping
8 oz. poppyseeds
⅖ pint (U.S. 1 cup) milk
6 tablespoons raisins (optional)
2 tablespoons honey
2 tablespoons sugar
6 tablespoons nuts, chopped (optional)
1 tablespoon candied peel (optional)
1 teaspoon vanilla
2 tablespoons margarine, melted

Prepare the dough as for gugelhupf and roll out as thinly as you can. Cover with a cloth and set aside

Crisp Haman's pockets

Poppyseed yeast roll

to rise while you prepare the filling. Put the poppyseeds through the mincer and then boil with the milk, raisins, honey and sugar. When mixture is thick, remove from fire and add the nuts, peel and flavouring. Cool and then spread thickly over the dough. Roll up like a jelly roll and put into a greased tin. Set aside, covered, to rise again for about 2 hours. Leave in a warm place, until double in bulk. Brush top with melted margarine or a diluted egg yolk and bake in a moderate oven (350°F. or Gas Mark 4) for about 1 hour or until golden.

MANDELBRODT
ALMOND 'BREAD'

Cooking time   35 minutes
To make   25 slices

You will need

5 oz. self-raising flour
pinch salt
4 eggs
7 oz. sugar
4 tablespoons oil
1 teaspoon almond essence
8 tablespoons (or more) chopped
   almonds
cinnamon (optional)

Sift flour and salt. Beat eggs and add the sugar, mixing well. Stir in the oil and almond essence.

Almond 'bread'

Work in the flour mixture and the almonds. Pour batter into a narrow loaf tin. Dust, if you wish, with a little cinnamon. Bake in a moderate oven (350°F. or Gas Mark 4) for about 30 minutes. Cool and cut into ½-inch slices. Arrange on a baking sheet and crisp for a few minutes in a moderately hot oven (400°F. or Gas Mark 6).
As this biscuit keeps well it is kept on hand for unexpected guests.

TORTE L'SHABBAT
SABBATH SPONGE CAKE

(Illustrated in colour on page 124)
Cooking time   1 hour

You will need

4 oz. self-raising cake flour, sifted
pinch salt
7 eggs, separated
grated rind and juice 1 lemon
7 oz. fine sugar
½ teaspoon cream of tartar

CREAM ICING (optional)

12 oz. margarine
7 oz. fine sugar
4 egg yolks
4 tablespoons brandy
3 oz. baking chocolate, melted

Sift the flour with the salt four times. Beat egg yolks until thick and slowly beat in the lemon rind, juice and half the sugar. Beat egg whites with cream of tartar and when eggs begin to stiffen gradually beat in the sugar. Fold egg whites into the yolk mixture and then fold in the flour, sifting as you go along. Pour into an ungreased pan or large tube pan and bake in a very moderate oven (325°F. or Gas Mark 2—3) for about 1 hour. To stretch the cake turn the pan over on a rack and do not remove until cool. The cake is usually topped with a sprinkling of icing sugar and sometimes also split and filled and topped with the cream icing which is made as follows:
Cream the margarine and sugar until fluffy. Alternate the egg yolks and flavouring, a very little at a time, and continue beating. Add the cooled melted chocolate and continue whipping. Spread on the cake.
Sabbath sponge cake is eggy and airy and very traditional.

PIE SHAMENET V'GVINA
SOUR CREAM CHEESE PIE

(Illustrated in colour on opposite page)
Cooking time   26 minutes

You will need

THE CRUST

8 oz. biscuit crumbs
4 tablespoons melted margarine or butter

THE FILLING

1 lb. 2 oz. white cottage cheese, sieved
⅖ pint (U.S. 1 cup) sour cream
3½ oz. sugar
2 eggs, beaten
1 teaspoon vanilla
2 tablespoons flour

THE TOPPING

⅖ pint (U.S. 1 cup) sour cream
2 tablespoons sugar
1 teaspoon vanilla

THE DECORATION

cherries or mint leaves

To make the crust mix the biscuit crumbs and margarine and pat into a spring pan. Chill.
To make the filling, mix all the ingredients and beat well. Carefully pour over the crust and bake in a moderate oven 350°F. or Gas Mark 4) for 20 minutes. Remove pie from the oven and turn the heat up to 450°F. or Gas Mark 8. Mix the ingredients for the topping and spoon carefully over the pie. Return the pie to the hot oven for just 5 minutes. Remove from oven. The topping sets as it cools. Trim with a border of cherries and mint leaves.

HONIK LEKACH
HONEY CAKE

(Illustrated in colour on page 124)
Cooking time   about 1 hour 10 minutes

You will need

⅖ pint (U.S. 1 cup) strong coffee
scant ¾ pint (U.S. 1¾ cups) honey
3 tablespoons brandy
4 eggs
4 tablespoons oil
8 oz. brown sugar
14 oz. flour
3 teaspoons baking powder
1 teaspoon baking soda
2 teaspoons mixed spices (chiefly cinnamon, with dash of cloves, ginger, allspice, nutmeg)
8 oz. chopped almonds, candied citron peel raisins, mixed in desired proportions

Mix coffee and honey, then bring to the boil and let cool. Add the brandy.
Beat the eggs, stir in the oil and sugar.
Sift flour, baking powder and baking soda and mix with nuts and fruits.
Stir the flour mixture into the egg mixture alternately with the honey mixture.
Pour batter into a greased loaf tin. Bake in a very moderate oven (300°F. or Gas Mark 2) for 30 minutes, then reduce heat to 275°F. or Gas Mark ½—1 for another 40 minutes. Invert the pan until the cake is cool.

Honey cake is the cake of Rosh Hashono.

132

Cottage cheese cake; sour cream cheese pie

A selection of jams and preserves

PRESERVES AND CANDIES

SUKARIYOT V'SHIMURIM

The celebration of Succot — the Feast of Tabernacles — was proclaimed in the Book of Leviticus, and ever since then a citron — the etrog — 'fruit of the goodly tree', has been used in the festival home service. Because of its shape the citron also became a symbol of the human heart and has been treasured for so long that in the Maccabean period it figured on Israel's coins. After the Succot festival the citron is often made into etrog varenje.

And what is varenje? It is a fine conserve, eaten with a small spoon along with a glass of tea containing a lemon slice. This delicacy was always given as a gift to the sick in our grandparents' day, and the well-wishing for health that went along with the making was: 'May this varenje never be given away.'

Candies in Jewish cuisine almost all have a symbolic link. Tayglach are made with honey for a sweet New Year; pomerantzen of Jaffa orange peel were so adored because the fruit was of the Holy Land that Yiddish songs and stories praised it. Mohnlach, a Purim sweet, sounds like 'Homan-lach' — 'Laugh at Haman' who was the villain caught in time to stop his planned massacre of the Jews. Candied almonds with raisins have many biblical associations — not only as food treats but for the beauty of the bud and bloom used to decorate the Menorah in the Sanctuary.

Home-made sweets such as ingberlach carrot candy, pletzlach apricot candy, are put out with lots of nuts on Passover. This is to replace manufactured sweets, for they would require supervision to ensure that no contact with any leavening agent took place in the factory. In Israel and New York — where Jewish communities are a market — such 'kosher for Passover' candies are available.

MIRKAHAT GUYAVA

GUAVA JELLY

(Illustrated in colour on opposite page)
Cooking time   45 minutes
To make   about 2½ — 3 lb. jelly

You will need

generous 1½ pints (U.S. 4 cups) guava juice
  (see instructions below)
1¾ lb. sugar
1 tablespoon lemon juice

TO MAKE THE JUICE
Select rather green guavas. Prick the fruit after washing but do not peel.

Cut into quarters and cover with water, about ⅖ pint (U.S. 1 cup) water for every pound fruit. Bring to the boil and cook rapidly for about 15 minutes.
Put fruit into a jelly bag to drain out for a few hours. Do not press the bag.

To the guava juice add the sugar and cook until jelly runs off side of a spoon in one sheet.
Add lemon juice and cook for a further minute. Skim and pour into hot sterilized jars.

Guava is so abundant in Israel that this jelly has become very popular.

RITTACH EINGEMACHTS
BLACK RADISH PRESERVES

Cooking time about 1 hour
To make about 1½ lb. preserves

You will need

1 lb. black radishes
scant ¼ pint (U.S. ½ cup) water
scant ¼ pint (U.S. ½ cup) honey
10½ oz. sugar
1 teaspoon ginger
8 tablespoons blanched almonds

Peel the radishes and cut into julienne strips. Cook for 5 minutes in about 2 pints water and then drain. Repeat and drain once more. Mix scant ¼ pint (U.S. ½ cup) water with the honey, sugar and ginger and bring to the boil. Add the radishes and cook over a very low heat until radishes are almost transparent. Add the almonds and continue cooking until the preserve is thick.

A traditional preserve of Passover among East European Jewry.

ETROG VARENJE
CITRON JAM

(Illustrated in colour on page 134)
Cooking time about 1 hour
To make about 1½ lb. jam

You will need

1 citron and 1 orange
equal weight sugar
water

Wash the citron and orange and cut them in half lengthwise and then very thinly slice them. Remove the seeds. Soak the fruit overnight. Change the water to cover the fruit and bring to the boil. Change the water again and bring to the boil once more. Pour off the water. Weigh the fruit and add an equal weight of white sugar. Cook over a low heat for about 45 minutes until the jam begins to jell.

The citron used at home in the Succot prayers as the 'fruit of the goodly trees' is treasured and after the festival goes into the making of this jam.

Citron jam

RIBAHT HADARIM MAHRIR
BITTER CITRUS MARMALADE

(Illustrated in colour on page 134)
Cooking time 2—3 hours
To make 8 lb. marmalade

You will need

1 Seville (bitter) orange
4 pomelos or 8 oranges (or part lemons) or 5 grapefruit or citrus fruits combined
8 pints water
5¼ lb. sugar

Use two saucepans — each to cook different parts of the citrus fruits at the start. Cut the scrubbed peel into very fine strips and cook separately with 4 pints (U.S. 10 cups) water for about 1½ hours until the peel is soft. Meanwhile cut up and boil the pulp of the fruit (be careful not to include the pips) in the other saucepan with the remaining water. Do not cover the saucepans and let the pulp boil rapidly. After the fruit has cooked for 1½ hours strain it through a very fine sieve or cheese cloth. The fruit pulp is not used further. The liquid from the pulp is transferred to the big saucepan with the peels. Boil for 5 minutes and then add the sugar. Continue to cook on medium heat until mixture begins to jell (it may take 30 minutes and it may take 1 hour, depending on the natural pectin in the fruit). Pour into sterilized jars.

You can use any citrus fruit alone or combined in this recipe. The Seville orange adds a delightful bitter note.

VARENJE TOOT SADEH

STRAWBERRY CONSERVE

(Illustrated in colour on page 134)
Cooking time   10 minutes
To make   about 3 lb. conserve

You will need

2 lb. strawberries
2 lb. 10 oz. sugar
juice 3 lemons

Hull and wash the strawberries and then layer them with the sugar. Set aside in the refrigerator overnight. Pour off the liquid and cook it over a high heat for about 5 minutes, then add the strawberries and cook for a further 5 minutes. Add lemon juice; cook for another minute. Seal in sterilized jars. As strawberries are harvested at Passover time in Israel, this has become a festive jam.

MIREIHAT LIMON

LEMON CURD

Cooking time   about 10 minutes
To make   about 1½ lb. curd

You will need

3 eggs
3 oz. butter
7 oz. sugar
rind and juice 2 lemons

Slightly beat the eggs, add the butter, sugar and lemon rind and juice. Put into top of a double saucepan and stir until mixture is thick and smooth. Pour in warm jars and cool before refrigerating.

POVIDL

PLUM JAM

(Illustrated in colour on page 134)
Cooking time   about 45 minutes
To make   about 3 lb. jam

You will need

2 lb. purple plums, washed and stoned
scant ¼ pint (U.S. ½ cup) water
2½ lb. sugar

Put plums into a heavy saucepan with the water and cook until fruit is very soft. Put the fruit through a sieve and add the sugar. Cook over medium heat, stirring often, until the mixture is thick.
Used particularly on Purim, among communities from Central Europe.

RIBAHT HAZILIM
OH KISHUYIM

SQUASH OR AUBERGINE JAM

Cooking time   about 1½ hours
To make   about 3 lb. jam

You will need

2 lb. very small summer squashes or tiny
   aubergines
2 lb. sugar
8 tablespoons pecans, pistachio nuts or walnuts
   (optional)
orange essence or other flavouring
If tiny vegetables are not available, the squash or aubergine can be diced.

Put the small vegetables, whole and unpeeled, into a heavy saucepan with the sugar and cook over low heat for about 1½ hours or more until mixture is thick. Add the broken nuts and flavouring and cook 5 minutes more.

A treat in North-African Jewish homes.

Squash jam

RIBAHT KUMQUATIM
KUMQUAT PRESERVES

(Illustrated in colour on page 134)

Cooking time　about 45 minutes
To make　　about 2 lb. preserves

You will need

1½ lb. kumquats
scant 1 pint (U.S. 2¼ cups) water
10½ oz. sugar
generous ¼ pint (U.S. ¾ cup) honey

Wash but do not peel the kumquats. Make a small incision at the tip of each kumquat. Bring the water, sugar and honey to the boil. Add the kumquats. Cook for about 1 hour over low heat until kumquats become almost transparent. Cool and then put into jars.
Eaten with a spoon and a glass of lemon tea, as a varenje.

RIBAHT SHOSHANIM
ROSE JAM

Cooking time　about 30 minutes
To make　　about 2½ lb. jam

You will need

1 lb. red rose petals
1 lb. lemons
water
1 lb. sugar

Trim off the white tip at the heart of the rose petals. Cut lemons paper thin, cover with water and bring to the boil. Drain. Add the sugar, rose petals and 2 tablespoons water and cook until mixture is thick.
Traditionally used in Persian homes on Shavuot.

RIBAHT TAPUZIM
ORANGE JAM

Cooking time　about 1½ hours
To make　　about 7 lb. jam

You will need

4 lb. Jaffa oranges
juice 4 more oranges
4 lb. sugar

Wash and peel the oranges and cut peels into squares. Boil peel four times in changes of water. Dice the fruit. Add peel, juice and sugar to the diced fruit and cook over a low heat until mixture is thick. Pour into sterilised jars.
Note
If you prefer, you can put the boiled peel and the orange pulp through the mincer for a different texture.
Made in almost every Israeli farmer's kitchen.

METTIKA-GLEECOA
QUINCE OR APPLE CONFITURE

Cooking time　20—45 minutes
To make　　about 2½ lb. confiture

You will need

2 lb. quinces or apples
water
7 oz. sugar
⅖ pint (U.S. 1 cup) honey or syrup
1 teaspoon rose water or vanilla essence
juice 2 lemons

Peel and cut the fruit into cubes. Parboil them in enough water to cover. Add remaining ingredients and cook until fruit is done. Quinces will need about 40 minutes and apples about 15 minutes till cooked.
An Iraqi and Greek confiture that is used instead of apples and honey on the Rosh Hashono board.

RIBAHT SHAZIFIM
DAMSON JAM

Cooking time　about 45 minutes
To make　　about 4 lb. jam

You will need

2 lb. damsons
¾ pint (U.S. scant 2 cups) water
2½ lb. sugar

Wash the damsons and place them in a saucepan with the water.
Cook the fruit gently until it is tender (about 30 minutes). Add the sugar, bring to the boil and boil for about 15 minutes, stirring all the time.
Test and then pour into warm, dry jars.

MOHNLACH

POPPYSEED CANDIES

Cooking time   about 10—15 minutes
To make   about 24 candies

You will need

4 oz. blanched almonds
8 oz. honey
8 oz. poppyseeds

Blanch the almonds and drain. Boil the honey and poppyseeds and drop in the nuts when mixture begins to thicken. Candy is removed from fire when a soft ball is formed by dropping a little of the mixture into cold water. Stir from time to time. Pour on to a wet board till ½-inch thick. Cut into diamonds and let the candy harden before removing from board.
The traditional candy of Purim.

SUKARIYOT SUM-SUM

SESAME SEED CANDIES

(Illustrated in colour on page 143)

Cooking time   about 15 minutes
To make   about 35 candies

You will need

⅖ pint (U.S. 1 cup) honey
7 oz. sugar
6 tablespoons water
15 oz. sesame seeds

Bring the honey, sugar and water to the boil and then cook on a low heat, without stirring. When the liquid forms a ball in a glass of cold water stir in the sesame seeds and cook only until the seeds begin to turn light gold. Pour on to a wet board, cut into diagonals and let the candies harden.

PLETZLACH

APRICOT CANDIES

Cooking time   about 30 minutes
To make   about 35 candies

You will need

1 lb. dried apricots
water
1 lb. sugar

Overnight soak apricots amply covered in water. Cook the fruit until soft in this water and then put it all through a sieve. Add the sugar and cook — stirring often — until mixture forms a soft ball in cold water. Pour on to a wet board and when cool cut into quadrangles.

A sweet of Passover and other festivals.

FISTOOKIS-GARINIM

TOASTED SEEDS

Cooking time   2—3 hours

You will need

sunflower, pumpkin, melon or watermelon seeds
water
about 2 teaspoons salt to each ⅖ pint
(U.S. 1 cup) water

Put the seeds into salted water and bring to the boil, then lower the heat and simmer for about 1½ hours. Drain the seeds well and then put them in a very slow oven (250°F. or Gas Mark ¼—½) stirring every 15 minutes until seeds are crisp. This takes from 40 minutes to 1½ hours, depending on the seed.

Oriental and East-European communities nibble these at festive occasions.

Toasted seeds

PAHT HAR SINAI
MOUNT SINAI MARZIPAN

Cooking time   about 10 minutes
To make   about 18 pieces

You will need

12 oz. almonds
5 oz. sugar
3 eggs, separated
rind 1 lemon or orange
2¼ oz. icing sugar
1 tablespoon hot water
½ teaspoon lemon juice
candy confetti

Blanch and grind the almonds and mix with the sugar. Beat the egg whites and add to the almonds to make a paste, then add the yolks and the grated lemon rind. Cook mixture in top of double saucepan, stirring all the time, until mixture is thick. Cool and form into cones to look like a mountain. Refrigerate for 30 minutes. Mix the icing sugar with the hot water and lemon juice and ice the marzipan. Decorate with coloured candy confetti or chocolate flakes to resemble the cloud over Mt. Sinai.

ROZINKIS MIT MANDLEN
RAISINS AND ALMONDS

You will need

raisins and almonds

Mix together and serve as a sweet (not at meals). This is so Jewish that folksongs have been written about it.

POMERANTZEN
CANDIED CITRUS PEEL

(Illustrated in colour on page 143)
Cooking time   about 1 hour
To make   about 1½ lb. candied peel

You will need

6 Jaffa oranges or grapefruits
   (or equivalent size of the other citrus fruits)
1 lb. 5 oz. sugar
generous ½ pint (U.S. 1½ cups) water
juice 1 lemon

If you use other citrus fruits, weigh the peel and use an equal weight of sugar, and for water use half the quantity measure of the sugar. Wash and wipe the fruit. Remove skins in sections. Cut peel into strips. Cover with water and bring to the boil. Change water and boil again and again (six times is the best). Drain. Put in the sugar and water and cook slowly until all the syrup has been absorbed. Add the juice of one lemon and stir. Drain and roll the peels in sugar. Let dry on a rack for a day or two before serving.

TAYGLACH
HONEYED CONFECTION

Cooking time   about 35 minutes
To make   about 36 pieces

You will need

2 eggs
7 oz. self-raising flour
pinch salt
⅖ pint (U.S. 1 cup) honey
5 oz. sugar
2 teaspoons ground ginger
6—8 oz. chopped nuts, any kind

Slightly beat the eggs, and then work in the flour and salt. Roll out into ropes of ½-inch diameter and cut into ½-inch pieces. Put the honey, sugar and ginger into a saucepan and bring to the boil.

Honeyed confection

Drop in the pieces of dough, about a fourth of the batch at a time. Reduce the heat and cook for about another 30 minutes without stirring. Pour on to a wet board upon which the broken nuts have been sprinkled. Cool; cut into rectangles or make mounds of the Tayglach and let them dry.

RAHAT HALKUM
TURKISH DELIGHT

Cooking time   about 20 minutes
To make   about 24 pieces

You will need

5 tablespoons cornflour
scant ¼ pint (U.S. ½ cup) cold water
scant ¼ pint (U.S. ½ cup) hot water
14 oz. sugar
scant ¼ pint (U.S. ½ cup) orange juice
2 tablespoons lemon juice
1 teaspoon rose water
3 oz. pistachios or almonds, chopped
2 drops red food colouring (optional)
icing sugar

Dissolve the cornflour in the cold water and set aside. Bring the hot water, sugar and orange juice to the boil and then stir in the cornflour mixture. Cook over a very low heat, stirring continuously for about 15 minutes. Remove from fire and stir

in the lemon juice, food colouring, flavouring and nuts. Just heat to boiling point and stir well. Pour into buttered dishes (about 1 inch high), and when cold and solidified cut into cubes with a knife dipped into hot water. Roll the cubes in icing sugar.

The delight of all Mediterranean Jews who also use it in pastries.

INGBERLACH
CARROT CANDIES

Cooking time   about 40 minutes
To make   about 24 candies

You will need

1½ lb. carrots, cooked and mashed
14 oz. sugar
1 teaspoon ginger or more, to taste
5 oz. blanched almonds, chopped
juice 2 lemons
sugar for sprinkling

Add sugar, ginger, and chopped almonds to carrots. Cook for about 15—20 minutes over low heat until thick, stirring occasionally. Add lemon juice. Sprinkle sugar on a board and over it pour carrot mixture. Sprinkle top with more sugar and just before candy is hard cut into squares or diamonds.

A Passover sweet without leaven.

Turkish delight

Carrot candies

NAHIT

CHICK PEA NIBBLE

You will need

chick peas
salt

Soak chick peas for 12 hours or more. Cook in fresh water for about 1 hour, until peas are tender. Drain and salt and, if you wish, pepper generously. Serve cold, like salted peanuts on the Sabbath.

MITOUKAY-SOLET

SEMOLINA SWEETS

Cooking time   about 5 minutes
To make   about 12 sweets

You will need

8 oz. semolina
pinch salt
2 eggs
scant ¼ pint (U.S. ½ cup) water
2 oz. walnuts, chopped
4 tablespoons icing sugar
oil as needed
warm honey

Make a dough of the semolina, salt, eggs and water.

Thinly roll out on a floured board and cut into 2-inch squares. Pound nuts with icing sugar and put a little in the centre of each square. Fold over and pinch edges together. Fry in deep hot oil until golden, then drain. Dip in warm honey.
A Tunisian candy of Purim.

SHKEDIM MISUKARIM

CANDIED ALMONDS

(Illustrated in colour on opposite page)
Cooking time   about 15 minutes
To make   about 1½ lb. candied almonds

You will need

3 tablespoons honey
5 oz. sugar
5 oz. blanched almonds
dash cinnamon (optional)

Put honey and sugar into a pan over low heat to carmelize.
Add the almonds and cinnamon and stir occasionally. When candy forms a hard ball in cold water, remove from flame. Pour mixture on to a marble slab and cut into squares or break into desired pieces.
A treat of all Jewish festivals, particularly among Turkish and Greek communities.

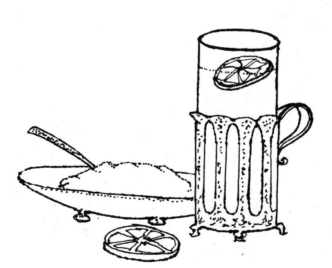

Candied citrus peel; sesame seed candies; candied almonds

Carrot baked pudding

PASSOVER DISHES

MA'ACHALEI PESACH

The Passover Seder — a religious ceremony and festive family dinner to which guests are often invited — recalls and celebrates our freedom from slavery in Egypt.

On the table, placed before the host (who sits among cushions to relish the comforts of a free man) are three covered matzos representing the unity of the three post-exilic Judaean communities — the Cohanim who were the highest religious authority, the Levites who administered and served the Temple's needs, and the Israelites — the people. The matzos are also symbolic of the bread of affliction.

The Seder dish has five symbolic foods upon it, some of which are tasted during the table ceremony before the dinner. A roasted bone — usually of lamb — symbolized the Paschal lamb. The charred egg represents the sacrificial offerings at the Temple.

The Haroset, a mixture of chopped fruits, is made to look like the mortar we laboured with in making bricks for Pharaoh. The horseradish, onion or other bitter herbs, are for the bitterness we suffered as slaves in Egypt. The celery, parsley or other sweet herbs are the agricultural symbol of the spring crops. A bowl of salt water for dipping the bibblers is in memory of the tears we shed in our captivity.

The Kiddush goblet of the host is for the blessing of the wine; another glass of wine is set aside for Elijah the Prophet. Wine for everyone is used in the ceremony, as well as the gala dinner.

Matzos replace bread on Passover because they are free of yeast. This biscuit was baked in haste on our flight from Egypt.

The Haggada — prayer book of the Seder—is read, discussed, chanted and sung before and after the dinner, making it a festive, memorable evening.

MAYEREN KUGEL

CARROT BAKED PUDDING

(Illustrated in colour on page 144)
Cooking time   about 1 hour
To serve   8

You will need

4 oz. margarine
8 tablespoons matzo meal
1 teaspoon baking powder
3 tablespoons potato flour
8 tablespoons wine
1 lb. grated raw carrot
2 oz. raisins
chopped dates (optional)
3½ oz. sugar (brown is best)
1 teaspoon cinnamon
juice and rind 1 lemon
1 egg, beaten
½ teaspoon salt

Cream the margarine and matzo meal and add baking powder. Dissolve the potato flour in the wine. Mix all ingredients together and bake in a buttered casserole for about 1 hour in a moderate oven (350°F. or Gas Mark 4).

A Passover dish that's good all year round.

HAROSETS
FRUIT MORTAR

No cooking
To serve   20

You will need

ISRAELI HAROSET

3 apples, peeled
6 bananas
juice and rind 1 lemon
juice and rind 1 orange
30 dates
8 oz. ground peanuts
⅖ pint (U.S. 1 cup) dry red wine
matzo meal, as needed
candied peel, if desired
2 teaspoons cinnamon
sugar to taste

OCCIDENTAL HAROSET

1 lb. grated apples
5 oz. chopped nuts
2 teaspoons cinnamon
dry red wine

YEMENITE HAROSET

30 dates, chopped
20 dried figs, chopped
4 tablespoons sesame seed
2 teaspoons ginger powder
dash of coriander
matzo meal as desired
dry red wine
1 chilli pepper (optional)

MIDDLE EASTERN HAROSET

2 oz. pine nuts (snobar or pinognes)
2 hard-boiled egg yolks
1 apple, grated
3 oz. almonds, ground
3½ oz. sugar
juice and rind 1 lemon
cinnamon and allspice
3 oz. raisins

All fruits are grated or mashed or put through the mincer, mixed with the seasonings and wine, and if necessary some matzo meal is added to stretch the amount and make it easier to shape into small balls or used as a paste on the matzo at the Service.

This symbolic dish, reminiscent of the mortar our people made as slaves in Egypt, is prepared differently by Jewish communities all over the world. The Israeli type makes a luscious dessert or delightful appetizer, depending on how sweet or piquant you make it.

ROTEV YAYIN
WINE SAUCE

Cooking time   about 10 minutes

You will need

scant ¼ pint (U.S. ½ cup) sweet red wine or
⅛ pint (U.S. ⅓ cup) cherry liqueur and enough
   water to make scant ¼ pint (U.S. ½ cup)
scant ¼ pint (U.S. ½ cup) water
1 teaspoon potato flour
5 oz. sugar
2 eggs
1 tablespoon lemon juice

Mix the wine or liqueur with the water and dissolve the potato flour in it. Add sugar and heat to boiling point. Beat the eggs and slowly whip in the hot mixture. Add lemon juice. Cook over hot water, stirring constantly, until mixture thickens. Serve hot or cold over dessert.

MINAS TAPUDIM-BEZALIM
MINAS OF POTATOES AND ONIONS

Cooking time   40 minutes
To serve   6

You will need

generous ½ pint (U.S. 1½ cups) hot oil
6 matzos
2 lb. onions or leeks, cut up and boiled
1 lb. potatoes, mashed
6 oz. grated Katzkaval or other yellow cheese
6 eggs, beaten
salt and pepper to taste

Put half of the hot oil into a casserole and then line the bottom and sides with half the matzos, dipped in water to soften them slightly. Put in the leeks and onions, mixed with the mashed potatoes, salt and pepper, and 2 oz. grated cheese. Sprinkle 2 oz. cheese on this filling. Cover with remaining softened matzos and then pour on remaining hot oil. Bake for about 20 minutes in a moderately hot oven (400°F. or Gas Mark 6), then pour on the beaten eggs. Bake 10 minutes more. Sprinkle with remaining cheese. Bake again for 10 minutes more. Pour the oil off immediately after the pan is taken out of the oven. It is best served hot but can also be served cold.

VARIATION

Instead of the potatoes and leeks you can use 2 lb. boiled spinach mixed with 8 oz. cottage cheese. The amount of yellow cheese can then also be reduced by half.

A favourite Turkish dish which is very savoury and hearty.

Cloud matzo meal dumplings in soup

LUFT-KNAIDLACH
CLOUD MATZO MEAL DUMPLINGS

Cooking time   30 minutes
To serve   6

You will need

6 oz. matzo meal
generous ¼ pint (U.S. ¾ cup) water
1 teaspoon salt
dash nutmeg or cinnamon or ginger
3 eggs, well beaten
6 tablespoons oil

Mix matzo meal with water, salt and spice. Whip in the eggs and then the oil. Refrigerate for half a day (otherwise the dumplings will not be light). Roll into balls and cook in boiling soup or water, putting in a few at a time. Knaidlach require about 30 minutes of cooking, but they can cook longer.

VARIATION

Knaidlach can be filled by inserting a little chopped meat mixed with finely chopped fried onion and seasoning. This is done by making a pit in each dumpling with your finger, filling the cavity and then sealing up the dumpling.

A fluffy dumpling for soup garnish or side dish to meat.

MATZO KNAIDLACH
MATZO DUMPLINGS

Cooking time   about 35 minutes
To serve   6

You will need

3 matzos
generous ½ pint (U.S. 1½ cups) chicken soup
2 small onions, finely chopped
3 tablespoons oil
salt and pepper
nutmeg or ginger to taste
1 teaspoon chopped parsley
2 tablespoons ground almonds (optional)
3 eggs
matzo meal as needed

Soak the matzos in the soup until soft and then squeeze them until all the liquid has been extracted. Fry the onion in the fat and beat up with the matzos. Add the salt, pepper and spice and stir in with the ground almonds. Beat eggs lightly and stir in. Add very little matzo meal but enough to just hold the batter together. Roll into balls. Set aside for about 1 hour. Drop into boiling soup or water and cook for 30 minutes.

These are quite different from the matzo meal knaidlach, but just as tasty.

Filled Passover pasties

CREMSLACH
FILLED PASSOVER PASTIES

Cooking time   10 minutes
To serve   6

You will need

THE PASTE

$\frac{2}{5}$ pint (U.S. 1 cup) water
scant $\frac{1}{4}$ pint (U.S. $\frac{1}{2}$ cup) hot oil
12 oz. matzo meal
5 oz. sugar
3 eggs
$\frac{1}{2}$ teaspoon salt
dash ginger, cinnamon or cloves

THE FILLING

14 oz. fruit preserves
8 tablespoons chopped nuts
about 1—2 tablespoons matzo meal

To make the paste, boil water and oil and pour over the matzo meal mixed with the sugar. Set aside for 30 minutes then add the eggs, one at a time, and beat. Add the salt and spices. Form into flat cakes. Prepare the filling by mixing the preserves, nuts and enough matzo meal so the filling is not runny. Put a spoonful of filling on each cake and fold over, then seal and pat flat again. Fry in hot fat until golden. Serve hot or cold, plain or with a wine sauce (see page 150).

The most popular Passover dessert.

MATZO KUGEL B'YAYIN
WINE MATZO PUDDING

Cooking time   35 minutes
To serve   8

You will need

8 matzos
generous $\frac{1}{2}$ pint (U.S. $1\frac{1}{2}$ cups) sweet red wine
water if necessary
8 tablespoons melted margarine
$4\frac{1}{2}$ oz. raisins
$4\frac{1}{2}$ oz. chopped nuts
7 oz. sugar
2 teaspoons cinnamon
6 egg whites, stiffly beaten

Wine matzo pudding

Soak the matzos in half of the wine to soften them. If the wine is not enough, add a little water. In a well greased casserole put alternate layers of matzos, sprinkled with melted margarine, mixed nuts, fruits, sugar and cinnamon. Put a layer of beaten egg white on top of each layer of raisins and nuts. Bake for 30 minutes in a moderately hot oven (375°F. or Gas Mark 5), then pour on remaining wine and continue to bake for a further 5 minutes.

INDEX

INDEX

152

INDEX